MID-CENTURY BRITAIN

MODERN ARCHITECTURE 1938–1963

ELAIN HARWOOD

BATSFORD

First published in the United Kingdom in 2021 by
Batsford
43 Great Ormond Street
London
WC1N 3HZ

ISBN 978-1-84994-686-5

A CIP catalogue record for this book is available from the British Library.

10 9 8 7 6 5 4 3 2 1

Reproduction by Rival Colour Ltd, UK
Printed and bound by 1010 Printing International Ltd, China

MIX
Paper from responsible sources
FSC® C016973

CONTENTS

4 Mid-century Britain

20 The Festival of Britain

36 Private Houses and Flats

100 Low-cost Housing

124 Education

154 Public Buildings and Memorials

176 Shops, Offices and Industry

214 Entertainment

244 Transport

258 Places of Worship

282 Footnotes

283 Index

288 Picture credits

MID-CENTURY BRITAIN

Mid-century modern is a term coined in the United States to describe architecture and design from about 1940 to the early 1960s. Used only a little during that period, it became popular when in 1984 Cara Greenberg published *Mid-Century Modern: Furniture of the 1950s*, an example of the design world taking the lead in reviving a fashion and bestowing its nomenclature as it had with Art Deco.[1] The name was quickly adopted to describe the flash hotels built along Miami's northern shore in the 1940s and 1950s, and as quickly reduced to 'Mi-Mo', also referring to Miami Modern.

British architects around 1950 had their own terminology. They spoke instead of the 'New Empiricism' or 'New Humanism' to describe a gentle modernism that was simple and functional but had decorative touches. In calling her ground-breaking survey *Contemporary*, in 1994 Lesley Jackson revived a name used in its day for buildings and interiors considered to lack intellectual rigour, usually well-meaning public buildings designed by junior borough architects with too many contrasts of materials, colours and planes. 'When I hear the word contemporary, I reach for my revolver,' quipped Theo Crosby in a manifesto for the counter-movement, the New Brutalism.[2] What he would have made of the term 'Soft Brutalism' used today for much of this architecture should perhaps remain unprinted. 'Mid-century modern' might be American, but it usefully describes the best design by a generation that was equally confident in architecture, furniture design and landscape, which included such international talents as Arne Jacobsen, Alvar Aalto, Eero Saarinen, Charles and Ray Eames and Marcel Breuer. Yet the phrase can equally be used of more modest but dynamic symbols of post-war affluence such as cafés and ice-cream parlours. There is (inevitably) a more specific American term for this – the 'Googie' style, taken from the coffee shop of that name in Hollywood designed by John Lautner in 1949 and used by Douglas Haskell of *House & Home* magazine in 1952 to describe the futuristic shapes, day-glo colours and neon synonymous with the diners, motels and drive-ins of suburban highways. Planning legislation and limited car ownership, especially among the young, ensured such developments remained rare in Britain; a motel built at Newingreen, Kent, in 1952 was listed, yet was demolished.

One name truly describes the architecture and design of the 1950s in Britain, and Britain alone: the Festival style, a reference to the great exhibition of British culture and manufactures held across the country in the summer of 1951. It marked the evolution of modernism in a country where neo-classicism and Art Deco styles had dominated public building through the 1920s and 1930s. These had adopted many details from northern Europe, particularly Scandinavia, and so too did the gentle modernism beginning to be seen by the Second World War. If the Festival of Britain marked the high point of this style's fashionability, it remained the dominant style into the early 1960s, surviving longest in libraries, town halls and entertainment buildings. Elsewhere it began to be refined, to become more measured and simple in its ingredients, reaching a minimal extreme with the development of curtain walling – whole facades of glass, aluminium and steel. Mid-century modern embraces all these variants. First of all, though, the use of the word 'modern' requires some extra explanation, taking us back further in time.

The Modern Movement

Britain saw little in the 1920s of modernism, the radical style epitomised by white boxes of reinforced concrete. It need not have been so, for the country had made early advances in concrete as well as steel-framed construction, just as its Arts and Crafts movement had looked for simplicity in the use of traditional materials and furnishings. Indeed, in his book on modernism first published in 1936, Nikolaus Pevsner claimed William Morris as its first pioneer.[3] Nevertheless, it would be possible to write a parallel account of early 20th century architecture in the English-speaking world, especially the United Kingdom, which focused solely on classical buildings. A genre harking back to the traditions of Sir Christopher Wren seemed suited to the head of the world's largest empire and responded to building regulations that favoured conservative construction methods; it was encouraged by the importation of Beaux-Arts doctrines from France to the growing schools of architecture, notably at Liverpool University, which in 1894 introduced the first course to be recognised by the Royal Institute of British Architecture (RIBA).

In the 1920s British architects found inspiration in northern Europe and especially Scandinavia. Denmark and Sweden also followed a broadly neo-classical tradition at this time, with Philip Morton Shand coining the phrase 'Swedish Grace' to describe the stripped-back refinement found in that country. Its builders developed distinctive brick bonds and diaper patterns, projecting headers being a particular favourite, which they combined with render and coloured tiles. Monopitch roofs were practical in heavy snowfalls. The Netherlands offered an extensive range of more modern housing models, from low-rise estates by J.J.P. Oud to tall flats by Johannes Brinkman and Willem van Tijen; Philip Powell and Hidalgo Moya used their student prizes to visit Rotterdam in 1945 ahead of designing Churchill Gardens. Willem

Housing at Römerstadt, Frankfurt: Ernst May, 1928.

Dudok's new town of Hilversum became a source for many public buildings. Herbert Tayler knew the Netherlands through his Dutch mother, but was also impressed by Ernst May's working-class terraces in Frankfurt, seen on a student trip with his partner David Green in 1930.

The development of reinforced concrete was taken forward in Europe and then America rather than Britain. The reinforcement of concrete with an embedded steel mesh provided some tensile strength and a greater efficiency in compression, and was first patented in Britain under franchise by a French company, Hennebique. The result in 1897 was an enormous flour mill for Weaver & Co. in Swansea. By 1914, architects in central Europe were showing that steel, glass and concrete could produce industrial architecture of great elegance, exemplified by Gropius's Fagus Factory at Alfeld near Hanover completed that year. Meanwhile, in Vienna, Otto Wagner, Adolf Loos and others were designing prestigious offices and executive houses without mouldings, producing geometric shapes with sheer planes as facades. After 1918, these

Bauhaus, Dessau: Walter Gropius, 1924.

clean forms, acknowledging only the basic classical proportions to inform new ways of interspersing solids and voids, suggested a stylish, healthier way of living – one without excess or the trappings of past regimes now discredited. This seemingly simple architecture also offered possibilities for cheap housing and a range of public buildings, addressing a social agenda of growing importance as left confronted right in the straitened times that followed the Great War and Russian Revolution.

The underlying theories of practicality and propriety *(Sachlichkeit)* and the spirit of the age *(Zeitgeist)* were largely published in German, although Dutch, Czech, Swiss, Russian and French architects contributed to the movement. While it established a course teaching architecture only belatedly, a centre for the movement was the Bauhaus, the art school in Weimar renamed by Gropius in 1919 and moved by him in 1924 to Dessau, some two hours south of Berlin. A meeting point for artists and designers from across Europe where the planes of Dutch *de Stijl* met the expressive forms of Russian constructivism, the Bauhaus also encouraged rigorous thinking from first principles and collaborations between architects and between them and other disciplines on an equal footing. No fewer than 17 architects contributed to the Weißenhofsiedlung, a housing estate in Stuttgart built as an exhibition for the Deutscher Werkbund in 1927. Of the 21 buildings erected using flat roofs and generally white exteriors under the direction of Ludwig Mies van der Rohe, 11 have survived. They include three houses by Le Corbusier (Charles-Édouard Jeanneret), in which he demonstrated the 'five points' that he felt underlay all modern architecture: the unmoulded column or 'piloti', a free plan, free facade, strip windows and flat roof. The requirements presumed a reinforced concrete frame supported on the pilotis, though in practice the outside walls – whether of concrete or brick – continued for a time to take much of the load. The following year, 1928, saw the Congrès Internationaux d'Architecture Moderne (CIAM) founded at La Sarraz in Switzerland as a forum for debating ideas on modern architecture that continued until 1959, charting the wider aspirations of the mid-century towards planning and urbanism, and eventually sealing the style's eclipse.

Britain had little building in this modern style before 1930. The first building in the style is generally acknowledged as New Ways, Northampton, a house of rendered brick from 1925–26 by the German architect Peter Behrens for W.J. Bassett-Lowke, whose career as a model engineer brought him in close contact with designers and toy manufacturers from that country. More telling was High and Over, erected in 1929–30 on the hill above Amersham, Buckinghamshire, by Amyas Connell, a New Zealander who had come to London with his friend Basil Ward determined to win the Prix de Rome in classical architecture only to be seduced by the work of Le Corbusier. Many of the earliest exponents of modernism in Britain came from the Commonwealth, with Raymond McGrath from Australia and

Wells Coates from Canada showing, like Connell and Ward, the benefits of travel and a broader education. They formed the core of the Twentieth Century Group in 1930 and the Modern Architecture Research (MARS) Group in 1933, which affiliated itself to CIAM. But when in 1932 Henry-Russell Hitchcock and Philip Johnson published *The International Style* alongside an eponymous exhibition at New York's Museum of Modern Art, they included from Britain only Joseph Emberton's Royal Corinthian Yacht Club at Burnham-on-Crouch, Essex, opened in 1931.[4]

The rise of fascism forced an exodus of modern architects to the Americas, Palestine, Africa and beyond. The westwards shift of CIAM, which left Le Corbusier in Paris as its dominant force, was exemplified by the career of a fellow Swiss, its secretary Sigfried Giedion. Born in Prague and educated in Vienna and Munich, from the late 1930s to the late 1950s he taught at Harvard University alongside Josep Lluís Sert, whose own exile took him from Barcelona through Paris to the United States. London was an important stopping point for many architect migrants. Some, like Berthold Lubetkin from the Soviet Union, settled permanently and supported later refugees such as Peter Moro, whom he employed as a specialist in staircases at his second block of flats in Highgate, Highpoint II. This block has a wider structural significance, for while the earlier Highpoint I of 1933–35 closely resembled the Weißenhofsiedlung in its structure (and was admired by Le Corbusier), at Highpoint II in 1936–38 the Danish émigré engineer Ove Arup made a braced frame from the internal cross walls and floor plates. This open-ended structure can be likened to a wine rack, a series of cubes with no front or back; because the central part of the main elevation carried no load Lubetkin could introduce double-height windows towards Highpoint's gardens. Arup refined this 'box-frame' in the 1940s, but even the simplest cross-wall construction made possible the lighter, open facades found in all post-war buildings from terraced housing to office towers.

The émigré architects Erich Mendelsohn, Walter Gropius and Marcel Breuer produced a handful of buildings in Britain before finding greater opportunities in the United States. Mendelsohn created the De La Warr Pavilion in Bexhill, opened in 1935, and Gropius a school at Impington, near Cambridge, a light, largely single-storey building of brick very different to the futuristic Bauhaus. To gain work permits, many émigrés formed partnerships with British nationals, bringing experience and kudos to a younger generation. These included F.R.S. Yorke, who had already promoted modernism – and his own career – with a book, *The Modern*

Weißenhofsiedlung, Stuttgart: houses by Le Corbusier, 1927.

House, which went through six editions.[5] In 1935–37, he formed a partnership with Marcel Breuer that saw the building of a white concrete summer house on pilotis at Angmering-on-Sea, Sussex, and alterations to Wells Coates's Lawn Road flats.

Mid-century Modernism

By the late 1930s these architects had learned that concrete and flat roofs were less flexible than they had hoped. Yorke's assistant Randall Evans recalled to the historian Alan Powers the problems of threading ducts and services through a roof slab at a house in Lee-on-the-Solent, Hampshire. 'Let's make a New Year resolution – no more concrete houses,' they had declared.[6] In 1936 Breuer produced a temporary pavilion of Cotswold stone for the furniture retailers P.E. Gane, exhibiting at the Royal Agricultural Show in Bristol. Raised in Stratford-upon-Avon, Yorke understood Cotswold building traditions, but for Breuer international influences were more important, including Le Corbusier at the Villa Mandrot in 1931, Pavillon Suisse (1930–32) or in his own apartment in the Rue Nungesser-et-Coli (1934), where he combined natural stone with a concrete frame. A little brick terrace at Stratford-upon-Avon, built in 1938–39 with stone end walls and a monopitch roof, shows Yorke turning the synthesis into a new British modernism.

Brewery Terrace, Stratford-upon-Avon: F.R.S. Yorke, 1938–39.

How British architecture might have evolved but for the Second World War can be seen at the Impington school and in a series of houses built in the late 1930s. These include Overshot, near Oxford, by Godfrey Samuel and Valentine Harding from 1937, faced in brick and timber under a shallow-pitched copper roof; three brick houses by Mary Crowley of 1936 at Tewin, Hertfordshire, for her family and a friend, all with monopitch roofs that acknowledged her great love of Danish architecture; and Moro's eclectic house at Harbour Meadow, Sussex, completed in 1940. The most intriguing is perhaps Brackenfell in Cumbria, a small house and studio for an artist and collector built in 1937–38 by Leslie Martin and Sadie Speight that married brick, tile and local stone with expressive shapes and massing drawn from Russian constructivism, explored first hand through the couple's friendship with another refugee, Naum Gabo. This was an early example of a building also designed as a repository for art, which became a feature of the early 1950s. Many of the younger architects, including Samuel, Harding and Crowley, had trained at the Architectural Association School of

Architecture in London, where modernism came to dominate teaching from the mid-1930s and where in 1936 a new principal, Eric A.A. Rowse, allowed the students to collaborate in groups on larger projects with time to explore social, historical and planning issues rather than simply produce designs. The move encouraged the students to become still more politically motivated, drawing them initially into conflict with the AA's management, but after the war it became an integral part of the school's working as well as the beginnings of many professional partnerships.

Walter Segal, who arrived in London from Germany in 1936, sought 'a natural architecture' and this shift can be seen in many northern climates. Frank Lloyd Wright experimented with traditional materials in the service of modernism from the mid-1930s, famously at Fallingwater, while Alvar Aalto embraced the Finnish landscape and climate with a collage of stone, timber, steel, concrete and render at the Villa Mairea of 1938–39. Houses at Lincoln, Massachusetts, by Gropius and Breuer heralded a new style more responsive to nature and place by marrying local rubble walling with timber framing and painted boarding. It was an assimilation of New England traditions and the latest in American open planning with their experiments in (old) England; its promotion by Sigfried Giedion as a 'new regionalism' was timely for émigrés seeking to show their commitment to a new country. Some of these houses were illustrated in the *Architectural Review* in November 1939, along with ones by Richard Neutra and William Lescaze – the latter with a flying canopy supported on two sharply angled columns. It was, however, Breuer's own house at Lincoln, with its double-height living space and contrasting materials, which offered the clearest model for young British architects. Gropius made group working fashionable when he founded the Architects' Collaborative with his graduate students in 1938.

In Sweden, Gunnar Asplund turned from classicism to modernism when in 1930 he curated the Stockholm Exhibition, its temporary buildings adopting a functional style locally called *funkis*, enlivened by colour, pattern and works of art. Imaginative sculptures by Carl Milles became a feature of the city's streets and quaysides, preferred to commemorative representations of past dignitaries. This change was followed in 1932 by the election of a social democratic government, heralding an innovative welfare state based on insurance programmes for the sick, elderly and unemployed (modelled on David Lloyd George's reforms in Britain), partial nationalisation and decent housing. The development of an architectural expression for this democratic socialism made the country particularly appealing to young, left-leaning architects from Britain.

Post-War Building

Construction in Britain, so slow through the 1920s and 1930s, picked up from 1936 but halted again with the outbreak of war in September 1939. The Ministry of Works and Buildings assumed control of building materials, especially timber, and continued similar measures into peacetime. This rationing was a bitter blow to the ambitions of the Labour Government elected in July 1945, the first to win a clear majority. Its mandate to build a more equitable Britain, supported by decent national insurance and healthcare, with good homes and schools, was based on the principles set out by William Beveridge in a government report of December 1942 that was read by a remarkable number of people. Aneurin Bevan, the dynamic young minister responsible for health and housing, was anxious to build. But supplies of softwoods from Scandinavia were decimated by a drain on Britain's dollar reserves in July 1947, following the end of an American loan, although luxurious hardwoods from the

Empire remained available because they could be bought with sterling. Controls on the profits of developing land or 'betterment', introduced in 1947 by the Labour Government, delayed the building of private houses and commercial offices – although it did not stop entrepreneurs from buying up sites ahead of the repeal of the controls by the Conservatives, who returned to power in 1951. The new government retained a system of licensing until November 1954, so that the limited supplies were directed towards schools, public housing and industry. This did not relieve the slow pace of most public building, which frustrated the efficacy of progressive legislation on new towns, planning and the National Health Service. More effective was the building of hundreds of new power stations and deep mines to meet rising demand for electricity and coal following Labour's nationalisation of the power and transport industries.

The shortages of brick and timber encouraged architects to be creative. The RIBA promoted prefabrication in an exhibition, *Rebuilding Britain*, at the National Gallery in February 1943, followed by ones on Swedish factory-made housing and new American townships in 1944. Timber houses were imported from Sweden in 1945–46, but of greater impact was the work of the Burt Committee and an Experimental Building Department that authorised the building of thousands of two-storey houses using unconventional materials, many of which survive today. Between 1946 and 1951 the British Iron and Steel Federation erected 31,320 houses to a design by Frederick Gibberd that used sheet-steel panels as a distinctive cladding to lighten the upper storeys. Estates of these houses were commonly termed 'tin towns'. Other manufacturers used precast concrete beams or slabs, sometimes with brick end walls; of these, Cornish Unit housing using the waste from china clay manufacture can be

Swedish prefabs, Auckley, Doncaster, c. 1948.

most easily identified because the upper floor is set in a mansard roof.

The quintessential 'prefabs', however, were the 156,623 small bungalows built under the Temporary Housing Act of 1944 after Sir Winston Churchill promised that half a million new homes would be built as soon as war ended. Willing inventors experimented with plywood, concrete and asbestos sheeting, producing 11 approved variants after the government's steel prototype – exhibited at the Tate Gallery in May 1944 – was found to be too expensive. For architects brought up on Meccano, wartime innovations and American experiments in packaged housing (by Konrad Wachsmann, Walter Gropius and Buckminster Fuller), these were exciting times. By 1948 bricks were back in supply and the cost of transporting precast units from several suppliers was competitive only for larger structures, making schools the one outstanding success of the prefabrication story. Large numbers of primary schools were needed quickly for new estates and to meet the baby boom of the mid- to late 1940s. Hertfordshire County Council's programme best captured the mood of the times, a development from first principles that brought together artists, engineers and manufacturers to create a bright, informal environment designed to stimulate the small child.

Sweden and Denmark promoted their brand of architecture and interior design aggressively after the war, publishing extensively in English. The *Architectural Review* devoted its issue of November 1948 to Danish architecture, which it later also published as a book, but Sweden attracted a greater number of architect-travellers, drawn to its social programmes and exhibition work as well as good design. Its neutrality in the Second World War ensured that its belated industrialisation and related housing programme continued through the conflict. Robert Matthew, chief architect at the London County Council, studied prefabrication and the concert halls recently built at Gothonburg and Malmö. However, its appeal was greatest among students and young graduates: Trevor Dannatt recalled the joy of visiting a country free of rationing and found a similar cornucopia in its architecture and design. Oliver Cox, Graeme Shankland and Michael Ventris lived in Stockholm for two months in 1947, which informed their work on housing and schools, while Ralph Erskine had already settled there permanently.

In the absence of building in Britain, and with the continued rationing of foodstuffs, clothes and appliances, exhibitions promising better days ahead assumed a great importance. Many architects, including Basil Spence, specialised in their design. An exhibition of new manufactures held at the Victoria and Albert Museum in 1946, *Britain Can Make It*, was popularly renamed 'Britain Can't Have It', since most new goods were directed to the export market in the vain hope of supporting the ailing pound. Devaluation in 1949 did little to relieve the austerity, made worse with the outbreak of the Korean War a year later. Fortunately, the greatest exhibition of them all – the Festival of Britain – was too advanced to cancel, although its budget was cut by a quarter.

The Festival of Britain

The idea of commemorating the Great Exhibition of 1851 was first suggested by the Royal Society of Arts in 1943 and revived in 1945 by Gerald Barry, editor of the *News Chronicle*, as a great trades and cultural exhibition.[7] A showcase for British advances in science, manufactures and the arts, it marked the country's move from the centre of an empire to focus on technology and innovation. The name 'Festival of Britain' was coined by Prime Minister Clement Attlee and Herbert Morrison, Labour's deputy leader. Yet, while the event was closely associated with Labour and Morrison's old stamping ground of the London County Council, which provided the three main London sites and built the Royal Festival Hall, its style was determined by Gerald Barry as director general and Hugh Casson as director of architecture. Casson (1910–99) typified a generation of architects trained in the 1930s whose career had been cut short by the war, but who now found a belated chance to build – and with a freedom to do much as they liked. A core group had worked with Casson on an exhibition for the MARS Group in 1938, and he asked friends he could trust to take on the central buildings and open spaces. By 1951 it seemed that nearly every architect in London was working on the Festival to meet its 3 May deadline.

Having so many designers led to a great complexity of detailing, despite simple materials and an intended life of just five months for the main exhibition on London's South Bank. The tight site was very different from the open plain of the Champ de Mars used for exhibitions in Paris, yet a twisting circulation route controlled by changes in levels, landscaping and water features worked to its advantage. It personified the revival of the picturesque movement in buildings and landscape which the editors of the *Architectural Review* (of whom Casson was one) had promoted during the war as a symbol of national identity and a contrast to the

The Festival of Britain, 1951.

straight lines and neo-classicism of totalitarianism, whether of the left or right. Articles on Capability Brown and the English public house had run alongside those on new architecture in Sweden and Brazil. By the late 1940s the movement had evolved into what the magazine's owner Hubert de Cronin Hastings had christened 'townscape', the picturesque weaving together of variously shaped buildings, hard landscaping and street furniture in towns old and new, generally to be explored on foot. The idea was taken forward by his art editor, Gordon Cullen, with articles in the *Architectural Review* that in 1961 were collated as a book, also called *Townscape*.

There were affinities between the Festival and the Stockholm Exhibition of 1930, in its relationship to water and constructivist juxtapositions, unified colour palette and lettering. A still closer association was with the New York World's Fair of 1939–40, which featured a circular exhibition building, the Perisphere, and a needle-like landmark tower, Trylon. The Festival of Britain had respectively the Dome of Discovery by Ralph Tubbs for its main exhibitions and Skylon, a cigar-like structure supported on a cat's cradle of cables devised by Powell and Moya with the engineer Felix Samuely. Its ebullient style was most clearly seen in the Lion and Unicorn Pavilion, by Robert Russell and Robert Goodden, probably from an idea by Casson (he certainly thought of the name). It was a whimsical celebration of British character based on the heraldic supporters of its coat of arms, one standing for 'realism and strength' and the other 'fantasy, independence and imagination'.[8] They were displayed as traditional corn dollies, while giant figures represented the law, church and *Alice in Wonderland*'s White Knight, set under a flight of plaster doves issuing from a wicker cage and symbolising liberty.

The Festival was the last great event before television became widely available, so people had actually to visit the South Bank to appreciate it. People braved the long queues and puzzling displays to enjoy the experience of being in a modern village in the heart of London, where the Gothic gables of Whitehall Court across the river added to the sense of folly. It came to life at night when, lit by tiny bulbs set in the concourse paving, hundreds of dancers defied the wet weather to foxtrot in their overcoats. The unseemly haste of the exhibition's demolition in early 1952 ensured its mythical status. The LCC were persuaded to clear the site quickly in the expectation that its development as a cultural centre, begun so promisingly with the Royal Festival Hall, would continue. Instead the government reneged on the deal and the land stood empty for a decade, when lines of trees and the imposition of covenants over certain views – as well as much larger buildings – ensured that the Festival's happy intricacy was not repeated.

The South Bank's centrepiece architecturally and culturally was the Royal Festival Hall, the one permanent building. A replacement for the bombed Queen's Hall, home of the London Proms, it reflected a revival of classical music in the wake of wartime concerts and radio broadcasts, seen too in the Aldeburgh, Cheltenham, Edinburgh and Malvern festivals, the Third Programme (now Radio 3) and the Arts Council – all launched in the late 1940s. But while there was little save praise for the RFH's auditorium and the great foyers that surrounded and underpinned it, the elevation with its patterns of little windows and mix of materials raised questions – already voiced internationally in a series of articles by Sigfried Giedion – about whether the mid-century modern style had the gravitas for a really major public monument.

The Festival Council encouraged every city, parish and county council to contribute to the event, mainly in the form of pageants, cricket matches and fêtes. Bedfordshire County Council erected new village signs and Lincolnshire installed park benches, both featuring Abram Games's Festival symbol of Britannia rising on a compass point from an ocean of bunting. Farmington in Gloucestershire and Thornhill in Cumberland were among many parish councils to erect bus shelters. York restored its art gallery and assembly rooms, and erected flats in Castlegate and Fishergate. Ellesmere Port, Cheshire, saw the opening of Festival Road (lined with traditional terraces) and Festival Park, while plaques appeared on new public housing from Gainsborough in Lincolnshire to the Cotswolds. The Festival's Council of Architecture made special awards to 17 post-war schemes, which it felt contributed to civic design and landscape, each commemorated by a plaque based on Games's symbol.

The Festival also opened pleasure gardens in Battersea Park, offering what Gerald Barry called 'elegant fun' alongside daring fairground rides from the United States. Although it was the Festival's flimsiest and most rapidly assembled element, it had the longest life, for the gardens reopened in 1952 and 1953 in a vain attempt to clear a debt of more than £1 million; the funfair continued until a fatal crash in 1972, finally closing in 1974. At the suggestion of Frederick Gibberd, a good friend of F.R.S. Yorke and Britain's most successful architect in the 1940s, a display of town planning was recast as a 'Live Architecture' exhibition, the rebuilding of an actual bombed area of the East End. Though it deliberately followed the scale and materials of its surroundings, the Lansbury neighbourhood was the first place in Britain where modern schools, shops and housing could be seen together. As the architect-turned-historian John Summerson commented, 'it is not exciting but it is important … the first realisation of a formula for urban re-development which appears to have great merit. Here, conceivably, may be the first step towards the redemption of our disgusting cities. Lansbury is unimposing but not unpromising.'[9]

What was the Festival's legacy? On one level there was only disappointment, with the loss of the South Bank and seemingly no end to rationing. Its left-leaning architects lamented the election of a Conservative Government committed to cuts in expenditure on schools and housing; even the new-town programme was threatened for a time. Many architects continued profitably in exhibition work, while others turned to designing shop fronts and coffee bars following the arrival of the first Gaggia machine in London in 1952. By 1960 there were over 500 coffee bars in the Greater London area alone, exploiting the low rents of the times, although most were decorated by amateurs. They catered for a wide audience in an era when most popular entertainment did not rely on alcohol, with late opening, jukeboxes and modern design making venues particularly attractive to teenagers.

The Festival's legacy was greatest in planning and landscape, developing the *Architectural Review*'s theme of integrating 'contemporary architectural practice with 18th-century landscape'.[10] Lansbury had little influence in the rebuilding of London but a huge one in the new towns designated following an Act of Parliament in 1946, eight in the Home Counties, with one in Wales, two in Scotland and three in the Midlands and north of England. Many architects who had worked at Lansbury went on to the new towns, including Judith Ledeboer, Geoffrey Jellicoe and Frederick Gibberd, who repeated his pedestrian precinct as The Stow, Harlow, completed in 1954. The new towns also employed landscape consultants, then still a new profession. Sylvia Crowe, whose collaboration with Gibberd at Harlow lasted 25 years, commented that it was the first time that landscape designers enjoyed a near-equality with architects. In all the new towns can be found contrasts of paving and cobbles, and the picturesque grouping of low-density housing and trees, but Harlow is the finest of this first generation.

Casson reconvened a section of the Festival team to design interiors for the Time and Life Building, an exceptionally luxurious project made possible with American money and opened in 1953 to coincide with the coronation of Elizabeth II. They reassembled only once more, for the interiors of the Royal Lancaster Hotel in 1968. Other bomb sites were rebuilt only slowly. The best example is Central Parade, Walthamstow, a symbol of the town's regeneration after its main crossroads was hit by a V-1 rocket; though the design was made around 1953 the block of flats and shops was not completed until 1958, largely because of delays in securing a government loan. It bears the full regalia of the Festival style in its kitsch assemblage of brick, mosaic and tiles, a wavy canopy and a clock tower; heraldic plaques record the ancient families of the area beneath a resplendent borough coat of arms. This version of mid-century modern was considered insufficiently serious by many architects and was quickly consigned to minor public buildings, cafés and the seaside.

Public Art

Mid-century modern buildings made a feature of their artworks. While in Britain public art remained largely commemorative, the interwar years saw imaginative sculptures appear in the streets of Sweden and Norway, and in the United States the Public Works of Art Project launched by Franklin D. Roosevelt in

The Stow, Harlow: Frederick Gibberd, 1951–54.

The Festival of Britain Award for Merit plaque on White City underground station, London.

1934 hired 3,749 artists to produce 15,663 paintings, murals, crafts and sculptures to enliven its government buildings. Comparison with the decorative public buildings of fascist Italy is coincidental. In the late 1940s, when construction remained difficult in Britain, art provided optimism and gaiety at relatively little cost. A 'levelling stone' was a symbolic first gesture ahead of the reconstruction of Coventry city centre, as was the erection of Sir William Reid Dick's sculpture of Lady Godiva. In 1944, Henry Moore's *Madonna and Child* at St Matthew's, Northampton, brought modern art to a traditional-style church already noted for its fine music and worship. Sculpture added status to even simple buildings, as Barbara Hepworth showed at Hatfield Technical College.

The Arts Council was established in 1945–46 following the success of the Council for the Encouragement of Music and the Arts in promoting events around the country during the war – a civilian version of the Entertainments National Service Association. In 1948 an Act made it possible for local authorities to levy a 6d rate to build concert halls and theatres, facilitating the building of the Royal Festival Hall and Coventry's Belgrade Theatre, but the fine arts lagged behind. A London County Councillor and art collector, Patricia Strauss, proposed an open-air exhibition of sculpture as a means of encouraging modern art into Britain's streets and open spaces. The success of the first show in 1948 led to more exhibitions, in 1951 as part of the Festival of Britain and every three years thereafter until 1966. Many of the exhibits from these shows, held at Battersea Park or Holland House, found their way to Britain's town centres, parks and housing estates.

The LCC also began to specially commission art for its estates, schools and old people's homes, a programme formalised in 1956, and in 1957 it employed its own artists, William Mitchell and Anthony Hollaway. Hertfordshire County Council instituted a programme for its schools and the Harlow Art Trust was formed in 1952 to instil a sense of community and place by introducing works of art into the new town. The Co-operative Wholesale Society employed its own artists within its architect's department and British Home Stores commissioned Henry Collins and Joyce Pallot to decorate its shops with reliefs based on local themes. Works by Henry Moore, Barbara Hepworth and other leading sculptors became symbols of stylish modernity for more prestigious offices and stores.

The Apogee of Mid-Century Modern, 1951–63

The 1950s saw the British economy revive, fitfully but in a generally upwards direction, and reconstruction quickened its pace. Building licensing ended in November 1954, four months after the last food rationing. Until that time, the number and size of new private houses were strictly controlled and at times of greatest shortage in 1947–48 restricted to key workers. Architects produced designs that could be extended later, planning them asymmetrically so missing parts would not show and favouring bungalows for their lower cost, greater flexibility and easy relationship with the landscape. A million servants had quietly disappeared from British households at the start of the Second World War, finding greater independence in the armed forces and munitions factories, never to return. Without the need for privacy and encouraged by better central heating, living spaces were opened up into large rooms, which became brilliantly lit when the invention of float glass made possible much larger windows. The kitchen area could be defined by a semi-open dresser or counter, designed so that a hostess could talk to her guests or a mother watch over her children.

Marcel Breuer took these ideas further in a series of 'L' or 'H'-shaped 'binuclear' dwellings, which placed the living and bedroom areas in separate wings. Areas for children were separated from the quiet and tidy 'adult' parts of the house. Breuer set out his ideas in a temporary structure exhibited in the garden of New York's Museum of Modern Art in 1949, setting the main bedroom under the highest part of the sloping roof, accessed from a stair within the living space. Other houses placed the principal rooms on a first floor resembling a classical *piano nobile*, especially where a sloping site and/or distant views could be exploited. J.L. Sert adopted this picturesque idiom in Long Island, and Breuer's assistant Harry Seidler took it to Australia with the building of three houses at Wahroonga, Sydney, including the Rose Seidler House of 1948–50 for his parents.

Even after 1954 there were regular shortages of bricks, reaching a crisis in 1961–63. Steel remained expensive, and a system of using concrete to bridge large spans cheaply was imported from Europe. In the early 20th century, engineers in eastern Europe had found that reinforced concrete could span great distances if formed into cones or cylinders that gave a balance of tension and compression. The technique was developed in Germany in the 1920s and patented in Britain in the 1930s, but was widely adopted here only after the war. The wavy canopies at Walthamstow's Central Parade illustrate these thin concrete shells in their simplest form. They could also achieve large spans without support, making concrete shells ideal for the hundreds of new bus stations and garages built as motorised transport replaced trams and trolleybuses or catered for the growing trade in day trips and holidays. The striking advance in construction between the shells at Newbury Park bus station and Stockwell bus garage show how quickly the system developed. The Irish Government evolved a national bus network based on a new terminus, Busáras (bus building) in Dublin, built by Michael Scott in 1945–53 and perhaps the seminal mid-century modern building with its wavy roofs and mosaics. The bus drivers' canteen on an upper floor is particularly fine. Its engineers, Ove Arup and Partners, were also commissioned to build ten bus garages with shell roofs, of which only one – in the suburb of Donnybrook – was realised.

More complex arched shell structures were developed as silos, exacting structures because shifting loads such as grain, sugar or sulphates place exceptional stresses on a building. Where there was an opportunity for architectural expression, the shell could be curved in both directions, evolving into the hyperbolic

Busáras, Dublin: Michael Scott, 1945–53.

paraboloid with upswept opposite corners. These complex structures, somewhat resembling a fluttering handkerchief, were surprisingly easy to form since individual planks did not need to be bent. Félix Candela in Mexico and Oscar Niemeyer in Brazil had cast concrete into novel shapes to create shady interiors; in Britain curved and patterned facades were a means of maximising contrasts of light and shade from the country's limited sunshine hours, which received their ultimate expression in 1962–66 at Centre Point by Richard Seifert & Partners – on the boundary of mid-century modernism.

Curtain Walling

Schools were one area where lightweight steel frames were favoured for their quick assembly, and standardised components enabled local authorities to build large numbers to meet long-standing backlogs and the urgent demand for new places. The most ambitious programme was in Hertfordshire, where the county council worked with a Midlands engineer, Ernest Hinchliffe, whose patent glazing company had expanded into building huts for the war effort. By making all the components fit an 8ft 3in (2.5m) grid the buildings could be easily configured in any direction, with cladding panels and large windows an integral part of the system. The informal, colourful interiors were designed around the needs of small children. The brains behind the venture, the deputy chief architect Stirrat Johnson-Marshall, moved on to the Ministry of Education in 1948, where he developed Hinchliffe's system and those of other firms into multi-storey secondary schools and colleges of higher education. Only in Nottinghamshire was the early success repeated, where a similar steel frame with a lighter cladding was developed in response to mining subsidence. Its real success came when Nottinghamshire brought in other authorities with subsidence problems to achieve an economy of scale, leading to the Consortium of Local Authorities Special Programme. In Nottinghamshire the CLASP system was used for all public buildings, including additions to County Hall. Elsewhere, its most successful adaptation was for the first phases of the University of York, built in 1963–66; six standardised college buildings and three specialist teaching blocks were arranged picturesquely around a lake in response to soft ground conditions and the need for speed.

The steel frame took mid-century modernism to its most lightweight and minimal extreme. In the United States steel was always an economical option, especially where speed of construction was important. Slender sections were used in sunny south California for a series of houses promoted by John Entenza, editor of *Arts & Architecture*, between 1945 and 1962 to encourage young architects and increase magazine sales. These 'Case Study Houses' were open to the public for a month or so on completion and were extensively published, Julius Shulman's photographs becoming icons in their own right. In Britain, the *Woman's Journal* and *House & Garden* each promoted a 'house of the year' into the 1960s. The work of Ludwig Mies van der Rohe became synonymous with steel framing after he settled in Chicago in 1938. His influence can be seen at Alison and Peter Smithson's Hunstanton School, designed before they began to think of brutalism, and in the work of Basil Spence's right-hand man, Jack Bonnington, who in the mid-1950s made a pilgrimage to Mies's house for Edith Farnsworth at Fox River, Illinois.

If Britain lagged behind the United States in steel, it quickly pulled ahead in the development of glass and aluminium for construction. Aluminium smelting advanced rapidly in the late 1930s to meet military demands for aircraft, leaving an over-expanded industry that had to find new markets rapidly once peace came. In Britain it was used for housing and schools, and the Dome of Discovery with its diameter of 365ft (111m) was briefly the largest aluminium building in the world. Later it was used for aircraft hangars, as by de Havilland at Hatfield in 1952–54.

Meanwhile, the curtain wall, where glass or opaque panels could be slotted into a common steel frame extending right across an elevation, began to appear in the 1930s at modern factories such as Boots in Nottingham or Van Nelle in Rotterdam, and at Peter Jones's fashionable department store in Sloane Street. In most of these, however, the position of the floor plate across the facade could still be identified. Pietro Belluschi explored the possibilities of a lighter curtain walling using aluminium as early as 1943 in Portland, Oregon, where in 1948 he built a version as the 13-storey Savings and Loan Building. The same year Saarinen, Swanson and Saarinen built a glazed two-storey laboratory at Drake University in Des Moines, Iowa, using components from the British firm Henry Hope & Sons, developers of the 'windowgrid' system popular for schools and colleges. The breakthrough building, however, was Lever House, an office block of 1952 by Gordon Bunshaft of Skidmore, Owings & Merrill sheathed in green-tinted glass in Park Avenue, New York, that recast the city's covenants on set-backs as a slim tower set back from the street over a simple podium, partly raised on pilotis to give a little space back to the street. Mastic fixings were slowly replaced by neoprene gaskets, adopted from car windscreens by Eero Saarinen for his General Motors Technical Center outside Detroit; they first appeared in London at the *This is Tomorrow* exhibition in 1956. The term curtain walling was used for both complete proprietary systems and facades assembled with separately sourced bands of windows and spandrel panels. As the craze caught on, so British glass manufacturers, led by Pilkington's and by Williams & Williams, promoted their own complete systems internationally. They proved invaluable for laboratories and specialist workshops that needed a sealed skin to reduce noise and dust penetration, and everywhere projected a progressive, clean image, to which careful landscaping and perhaps a sculpture could add sophistication. In Britain the leaders in the design of curtain-walled buildings were Gollins, Melvin, Ward & Partners. The practice's Castrol House, completed in 1959, was one of the first tower-and-podium office complexes in London, but it had won a competition for a curtain-walled tower as early as 1953 – not offices, but a teaching building on a constricted site at Sheffield University, completed only in 1966. In the meantime it used curtain walling for colleges of education, notably at Scarborough in 1958–61, as did Basil Spence & Partners at Southampton University from 1955 onwards.

The End of Mid-Century Modern

By the early 1960s the opportunities for curtain walling seemed exhausted, especially where there was no air conditioning to counter its extremes of heat gain and loss. In the United States even Gordon Bunshaft moved to expressive concrete forms, seen in Britain with his buildings for Heinz at Hayes near Uxbridge. As buildings got bigger and services more sophisticated, so their elevations tended to become more slick and neutral. Broadcasting House in Copenhagen and Malmö's State Theatre (Stadsteater) suggested that there was no shame in elevations that were respectively bitty or minimal; nevertheless, Leslie Martin and his successors at the London County Council's Architect's Department ensured that in 1962–64 the RFH was recast in a bland blanket of stonework, from which only small areas of the individual tiling protrude on the side flanks. This same neutrality can be seen in the work of architects internationally, for example in the sleek late buildings of Alvar Aalto or Arne Jacobsen.

State Theatre, Malmö, Sweden: Sigurd Lewerentz and others, 1932–44.

In 1963 Candilis–Josic–Woods (job architect Manfred Schiedhelm) won a competition for an entirely modular, infinitely flexible 'mat' building at the Free University of Berlin that took his desire for neutrality to an extreme.

By 1960 the British economy was growing steadily and the rate of new building intensified. The expansion of existing university colleges turned to wholly new universities, more new towns were designated and slum clearance and city centre renewal accelerated. Local authorities took on more ambitious programmes, abetted by large developers who had steadily amassed portfolios in the previous decade while land was cheap, and by massive building contractors who had cut their teeth with housing estates and the first new towns. Anything seemed possible in the space age. But while men could circle the earth there were insufficient building workers to meet this pace of construction in Britain, and neither were there sufficient materials. One answer was prefabrication, whether of steel on a small scale for schools, or of precast concrete for housing estates. Mid-century modern and its rough cousin, the New Brutalism – as defined by Alison and Peter Smithson in 1955 as the use of natural materials honestly expressed – gave way to the epic-scaled brutalism associated with the term today. Elsewhere modernism became slicker, and nowhere is this better seen than at St Catherine's College, Oxford, one of Arne Jacobsen's greatest mature works, where the suppleness of his earlier architecture is joined by a greater strength. The charm of mid-century modern lingered elsewhere in small commissions, in private houses and some public buildings where the process of commissioning and construction was slow.

The Legacy of Mid-century Modernism

In 1987 the government redefined its listing legislation to embrace buildings more than 30 years old; Scotland and Wales had already begun to list some post-war buildings. The date was propitious, allowing historians to appreciate the architecture of the 1950s without having to consider the larger and more controversial brutalism of the 1960s. The joyous patterns, shapes and textures of mid-century modernism could at last be enjoyed in their own right. Contemporary critics had asked for a continuation of 1930s functionalism, yet this was an architecture that was popular at the time and which fulfilled the heavy demands placed on it. Its revival even had some influence on the gentle neo-modernism of the 1990s, when timber panels and pastel colours reappeared on new buildings. In a brief flourishing of public building, the foyers of the Royal Festival Hall were restored and Bankside Power Station was repurposed as Tate Modern. What had been so right at mid-century also suited New Labour and the millennium.

A Note on Listing

The listing system in England and Wales is based on grades I, II* and II for both buildings and landscapes, with just under 10 per cent of all listings in the top two grades I and II*. Scotland uses the grades A, B and C, with A roughly equivalent to I and II*, while Jersey's grade 2 is equivalent to an English grade II.

THE FESTIVAL OF BRITAIN

ROYAL FESTIVAL HALL

Belvedere Road, South Bank, London
1948–51; London County Council Architect's Department
Listed grade I

The RFH was a calling card for public architecture and British modernism at a time of world austerity. *The Times* asked how the Festival could be held without a concert hall, and the London County Council accepted the challenge on condition that the main exhibition was held on the South Bank. It was part of a larger master plan for the arts by Charles Holden, and Robert Matthew, the LCC's chief architect, raised the 2,900-seat concert hall – 'the egg in the box' – over the foyers to make it fit. The landward elevation was left uncompleted pending a second hall. Matthew determined the other facades, and a little tilework survives at the sides. The scheme was taken forward by Leslie Martin, who later led proposals for its extension and refacing in 1962–64.

Moro's hand is best seen in the surviving interior, designed with his former students. The building was originally entered from the sides, on two levels. The river front was devoted to a restaurant, on two floors linked by a spiral staircase. The foyer columns also recalled Harbour Meadow (see page 42), and an insistent logic separated every element with a flash gap. Moro designed the net-like carpet pattern, to which Martin added the dots, while the staircase balustrades were grooved for your thumb. In the auditorium, the balcony fronts repeated the cyma curves favoured by Berthold Lubetkin, and Robin Day developed the seating with the car industry. It was one of the first interiors in England to use fluorescent tube lighting for architectural effect.

LANSBURY LAWRENCE SCHOOL

Cordelia Street, Poplar, London
1949–52; Yorke, Rosenberg and Mardall
Listed grade II

Critics were generally disappointed with the Lansbury Estate, considered a wasted opportunity for modern architecture. The exception was the primary school built at the head of the shopping arcade. Replacing a bombed school, it was named after Susan Lawrence, an early Labour MP and a campaigner against poverty in Poplar in the 1920s.

Yorke, Rosenberg and Mardall was an international practice founded in 1944 by F.R.S. Yorke, who secured most of the school work. There is a standard 8ft 3in (2.5m) steel frame under the stone, brick and concrete, as they had already used at Barclay Secondary School, Stevenage. In the entrance hall a separate concrete structure, painted red, props a cranked, cantilevered staircase. Infants are on the ground floor and juniors above, their prominent assembly halls set one above the other. Behind, a complex plan allows natural light into the ground-floor corridors, inspired by another architect specialising in schools, Denis Clarke Hall, who had made a study following reports on children's eyesight.

Geometric tiles in green and acid yellow by Peggy Angus (1904–93) enliven the dining hall and entrance hall, the latter carefully restored in 2007. Angus was briefly married to the architect and critic James Richards, and her tiles (made by Carter's of Poole) became a feature of YRM's work (and others) after Yorke admired her lino prints. Tiles featuring smiling sun faces appear in the nursery school that was added alongside in 1952, the first nursery built by the London County Council after the war.

FIRE
EXIT

LANSBURY ESTATE MARKET SQUARE AND CLOCK TOWER

Poplar, London
1950–52; Frederick Gibberd
Clock Tower and Festival Inn listed grade II

Until Lansbury there was nowhere in England with a contiguous group of buildings to demonstrate the rebuilding of post-war Britain on modern lines, fervently discussed since Donald Gibson had first expounded his plan for rebuilding Coventry in late 1940.

Proposals for an exhibition of architecture and town planning as part of the Festival of Britain were approved in February 1948. Frederick Gibberd declined an offer to oversee the whole South Bank site, but began thinking about the architectural display. In July 1947 he proposed that it be a 'live' exhibition: the rebuilding of part of the East End as one of the 'neighbourhoods' proposed in the County of London Plan. The site adjoined Chrisp Street, where a thriving street market was blocking an important thoroughfare. Gibberd built a new market square as part of a pedestrian shopping precinct, the first in Britain. Each range ends in a public house, including the Festival Inn, which retains its interior by R.W. Stoddart of Truman, Hanbury, Buxton & Co., complete with a mirror featuring the Abram Games 'Festival Star' logo. A pub sign based on the vertical feature at the South Bank, Skylon, is long gone.

The clock tower provided a tall feature and a statement of civic pride for Poplar, but funding delays saw it built only in 1951–52. Gibberd determined that it should also be a viewing tower (though it was soon closed because of the suicide risk), with two scissor stairs that start together but meet only at the top, inspired by the Château de Chambord in the Loire, France.

FESTIVAL PLEASURE GARDENS

Battersea Park, London
1950–51; James Gardner, John Piper and Osbert Lancaster
Landscape registered grade II*

The Festival Pleasure Gardens were London's Tivoli, and were briefly named after the Copenhagen fantasy. Battersea Park was chosen for its accessibility by river from the South Bank, and because the London County Council was willing to lease land for five years, necessary to make this commercial venture profitable. Ironically, many of the Festival structures intended to last the longest were the flimsiest: fantastic towers and grottos (many by the artist Hans Tisdall) were made of chicken wire and plaster.

Flower beds, fairy lights and fireworks proliferated, supervised by Russell Page. James Gardner orchestrated confections of sharawaggi and chinoiserie in mild steel and timber, including cafés and bars, a theatre, side-shows, and a tree-walk near the river, with Rowland Emett's scenic railway to the rear. Fairground rides arrived from America, but the Festival authorities promised something 'more restrained and less rowdy than a funfair', defined by the director general, Gerald Barry, as 'elegant fun'.

The one formal element was the Grand Vista, a sequence of pavilions and arcades, towers, terraces and gardens, lakes and fountains in its own sunken area. The artist John Piper admitted inspiration from 18th-century pleasure grounds and Regency Brighton, while the cartoonist Osbert Lancaster designed the Candelabra entrance, and gas-lit obelisks that sat in Piper's pools. At the southern end of the vista they decorated a firework platform with an image of the Crystal Palace. The water features were restored by Hilary Taylor & Associates in 2000, when simplified versions of Piper's structures were recreated.

DUNTON
19 51

FESTIVAL OF BRITAIN VILLAGE SIGN

Dunton, Bedfordshire
1951; S. Vincent Goodman, county architect

The 'Festival Star' was designed by Abram Games, one of twelve artists invited to submit an emblem for the Festival of Britain. The brief sought a design symbolising 'a summer of gaiety and good looks', and Games's was the clear winner – though he was asked to add the jaunty bunting to make it more festive. The logo adorned many official publications and souvenirs.

Games's image of Britannia within a compass rose reflected the intention of the organisers that it was to be a festival across all of Britain. A circular in 1949 invited every parish and town council to do its bit, by holding carnivals and cricket matches, erecting bus shelters or creating playing fields. Bedfordshire County Council was unusually ambitious, restoring the county's last working windmill at Stevington and converting Elstow Moot Hall to a museum of 17th-century life. It also resolved in August 1950 to erect signs in its 138 small towns and villages, chosen as having 'a lasting value' and being 'helpful, not only to visitors during Festival Year, but also to travellers in the county'. Many have been renewed, but some like Dunton are original (that at Blunham has been extended). They have rugged concrete posts (cast in February 1951) and wooden signs, with on one end the Festival logo and on the other the county's coat of arms, itself granted in April 1951. As most villages only got one sign, they tend to be found in the middle rather than at the entrance to a settlement.

219 OXFORD STREET

Westminster, London
1951–52; Ronald Ward and Partners
Listed grade II

It is unusual to find post-war offices and shops erected before November 1954 saw the end of building licensing, which directed Britain's limited supplies of building materials towards schools, industry and housing. The exception is the West End, where licences could be found for fashion showrooms, then migrating from the bombed area north of the Barbican. This narrow block, containing offices, a showroom and shop, is still more unusual for also being a surviving memento of the 1951 Festival of Britain.

The first drawings date from 1950. The developer Jack Salmon then began to make changes to his business, Oxford Street Properties Ltd, to support the rag trade. The design was revised in August 1951, when plaques of precast Carrara stone were incorporated into the facade. They depict (from top to bottom), the Royal Festival Hall with the shot tower and musical instruments, the Festival of Britain logo devised by Abram Games, and the Dome of Discovery and Skylon accompanied by scientific accoutrements. Their sculptor is unknown, but they are strong and crisp. They complement the banded metal windows of this corner composition.

This is a building transitional in style between the 1930s and the 1950s, designed by a firm that went on to work in every commercial style. It is a rare example of a post-war building recognised not only for its architecture but for its historic associations. It was listed when proposed for demolition, and instead its upper floors have been incorporated with those next door.

ZARA
HILLS PLACE W1
ZARA
ZARA
ZARA

LEONARD MANASSEH'S HOUSE

Bacon's Lane, Highgate, London
1957–59; Leonard Manasseh
House and sculpture listed grade II

Leonard Manasseh built three houses in Bacon's Lane, reserving the prime plot alongside Highgate Cemetery for himself. The problem was that he had five children but the council permitted only a two-storey house, so he inserted bedrooms into the high, asymmetrical roof. The first-floor lounge also extends into the roof, a double-height space raised over a kitchen-diner used for day-to-day living. Landings were kept small in the compact plan.

The exteriors, with their exposed concrete floor plates, hint at a brutalist expression of structure and materials, but Manasseh's demeanour was that of mid-century humility and sensitivity. The concrete is incised with a relief of a dove, an indication of his talents as an artist, while the bricks were salvaged from a Southgate church. Inside, the bathroom and lounge floors were tiled in marble from 74 Victorian washstands bought from a Portsmouth junk shop.

The direct connection with the Festival of Britain is in the garden. Manasseh won a competition for a restaurant on the South Bank, which was then cut from the project. He was left to design a small bar, set above the lavatories. His disappointment was eased by being allowed to commission a sculpture, *Youth*, from his friend Daphne Hardy Henrion. After the Festival it was set to go to the Arts Council's store at Langley Airfield, where it would have almost certainly been neglected and ultimately destroyed, but it was mysteriously rescued by Manasseh early in 1952 and now stands supreme in the garden, restored by his son Amos.

PRIVATE HOUSES AND FLATS

BRACKENFELL

Capon Tree Road, Brampton, Cumbria
1937–38; Leslie Martin and Sadie Speight
Listed grade II

Leslie Martin, prime mover of the 1950s, came to attention in the late 1930s with a series of houses and extensions, all in northern England and designed in partnership with his wife Sadie Speight. The two had met studying architecture at Manchester University before going on to teach at Hull. The contrast of simple classical proportions with constructivist incident, and of brick combined with a partly exposed concrete frame, makes the houses pioneers of the mid-century style. The largest, Brackenfell, also expressed a growing enthusiasm for the unity of the arts and architecture, for it was designed for Alastair Morton, a painter and the director of Edinburgh Weavers, then engaged in developing a sophisticated range of 'constructivist fabrics' designed by artists who combined modernism with a sense of English traditions. He was introduced to him through Ben Nicholson, with whom Martin and Speight were editing *Circle*, an 'international survey of constructive art'.

Brackenfell is a small house full of subtle ideas. It is of brick, but with porches built of local stone; the concrete of the various flat roofs projects as a series of planes. Inside the living rooms are a sequence of rooms facing south, while above is a large studio and sleeping terrace as well as bedrooms. Morton decorated the house with his own rugs, furnishing fabrics commissioned from Nicholson and others, and a fine collection of modern paintings. Here was mid-century modernism personified. The house has been carefully restored by the present owners.

THE STUDIO

Duke's Head Yard, Highgate, London
1937–40; Tayler and Green
Listed grade II

Herbert Tayler and David Green formed a partnership when in 1937 they were approached by the artist Roger Pettiward (also known as the cartoonist Paul Crum) and his wife Diana for a house and studio in Highgate. Pettiward's sister, Cynthia, had been at the Architectural Association, where Tayler had been the leading student of their year. They rejected a site in nearby Townsend's Yard in favour of Duke's Head Yard, behind the Pettiwards' existing house, where there was a coach house. This provided the footprint for a three-storey house, with a basement and roof terrace, and slowly the idea of a top-floor living and studio space took shape. Tayler divided the large space with low, built-in furniture that divided the live/work functions. To the rear a circular stairwell projects as a half-cylinder in careful brickwork.

The house looks modern, with its flat roof and long top-storey windows. Tayler and Green had visited Frankfurt as students, and the strip glazing of the top floor and bold framing to the lower windows (imported from Switzerland) owes something to mid-European design. Yet they adopted traditional construction using brick and render, as had Ernst May at Frankfurt, after Pettiward rejected Tayler's proposal for black bricks (a colour that reappeared in his later council housing). The house set a marker for mid-century design, interrupted by the war. Tayler produced a scheme showing how the design might be repeated as a terrace, but their post-war housing had perforce to be simpler and became more eccentric.

TIGUAN
2.0 TDI
LM63 ONH

HARBOUR MEADOW

Court Barn Lane, Birdham, West Sussex
1938–40; Peter Moro with Richard Llewelyn Davies and Gordon Cullen
Listed grade II

Harbour Meadow, overlooking Chichester Harbour, is a modern interpretation of a strictly private country house that looks forward to the 1950s. The roofs are flat, but the walls are of brick and stone as well as concrete, and many windows are boldly framed, a device introduced to Britain by émigré architects that became common after 1945. A 'Z'-shaped plan pushes the main rooms into a block overlooking the sea, separated from those for servants and children. Timber-lined columns in the morning room were repeated in the Royal Festival Hall, where the restaurant originally also featured an open spiral stair – a feature which at Harbour Meadow imparts a touch of Hollywood.

Peter Moro emigrated from Germany to Britain in 1936, after the discovery that his grandmother had been born Jewish frustrated his education, and secured work with Lubetkin and Tecton as a staircase specialist. He met the clients, George and Pauline Tawse, a Scottish steel manufacturer and his much younger wife, through his student flatmate, Richard Llewelyn Davies. When Moro could not attend site visits because of military restrictions around the coast, Gordon Cullen of Tecton took over supervision and contributed a Baroque framed window of coloured glass; this was as quirky a post-modern touch as Lubetkin's earlier caryatids at Highpoint II, London.

Moro and his assistant Walter Greaves restored the house in 1951 and designed a second house – realised by Greaves, who married the Tawses' daughter Annabel. Harbour Meadow was restored by Avanti Architects in c. 2007.

NEW HOUSE

Bracken Dell Road, Luccombe, Isle of Wight
1946–47; F.R.S. Yorke

Building licences after 1945 limited new private houses to key workers such as doctors and clergymen. The wily Yorke, an architect in the vanguard of the Modern Movement with Marcel Breuer in the 1930s, successfully argued that his holiday home trialled a new technique for building concrete foundations in an area prone to land slippage. More striking is the use of local stone within the concrete frame for the end bays, pioneered in modern British architecture by Breuer with an exhibition pavilion for the furniture manufacturer Crofton Gane in 1936, but harking back ultimately to Le Corbusier's Villa Mandrot of 1931 and Maison de Weekend of 1935. Yorke first adopted the idiom with housing at Stratford-upon-Avon in 1938.

The long central section, behind a long balcony, is timber-framed. Yorke's wife Thelma determined the linear plan that gives every room a view of the sea, though much of the detailed work was by his assistant Penelope Whiting. It was Thelma who demanded the house be sold in 1948, either for lack of money or because it was being misused by the office as a weekend retreat. The district nurse, Miss Triggs, cherished it for many years, as have the present owners. Because so many little houses of this period have been demolished because of their valuable sites, this is a remarkable survival. Yorke did produce versions of the house for caretakers at schools in Stevenage and Kidderminster, designed with his new practice Yorke, Rosenberg and Mardall, but in brick.

MARTINS

Toys Hill, Brasted, Kent
1954; Powell and Moya
Listed grade II

Powell and Moya built several tiny houses for their families, but all have been demolished. Fortunately their finest dwelling survives very little altered, quirky and engaging. Ian McCallum, an editor on the *Architectural Review*, recommended the architects (known mainly for Skylon and their rational, sophisticated university buildings from the 1960s) to his friends Monica and Muriel Anthony. Spinster sisters, they were businesswomen who wanted a weekend retreat for 'peace, privacy and a breath of fresh air'.

The site is an open, south-facing hillside. A garage and first-floor box room occupy the one flat site by the road, cedar boarding giving dignity to their unusual prominence. The rest of the house lollops gently down the hillside, angled towards a spectacular view across the Weald. It looks complex, but is essentially two linked single-storey pavilions set across the contours, simple boxes save for the jaunty brick chimney. One houses the living room, given added height by being set down steps from the separate dining room and kitchen under a common flat roof. Built-in bookcases resemble those installed by Powell in his modernised Kensington villa. Contemporary accounts describe the kitchen as large, for both sisters enjoyed cooking, though it seems quite modest by modern standards. The bedroom wing to the east gave each sister an identical room overlooking the view.

Martins is simple, built while licensing restricted building materials, but its disjointed, constructivist profile and fine internal finishes create a sense of enjoyment.

22 AVENUE ROAD

Leicester
1954–55; Fello Atkinson and Brenda Walker of James Cubitt and Partners
Listed grade II

Herald Goddard, manufacturer of metal polish, was a well-travelled businessman and an admirer of modern art and architecture. When in 1953 he and his wife Joan commissioned a new house in an old orchard, building restrictions constrained them to a floor area of 1,500 sq. ft (140 sq. m). They decided not to waste space on stairs, and encouraged the architects to create a free-flowing plan without prescribed circulation areas. The result is an early and rare surviving example of American planning on a modest scale, recently immaculately restored down to the original shades of bright yellow and duck-egg blue.

The house hugs the road to maximise the garden, forming an 'L' plan around a patio and surviving fruit trees. At its heart is the open-plan living room, connected via a hatch to the galley kitchen (facing the road) with on one side the 'adult' spaces – an office area, the master bedroom and garage – and on the other a long wing with the only corridor housing bedrooms for the children and guests. Atkinson and Walker returned to add a playroom in c. 1960. The house retains a Westmorland slate fireplace, which balances a panelled wall, along with built-in drop-fronted desks and shelf units, some of cherry wood – while the cupboards to the kitchen and hatch area are yellow and orange. The generous full-height doors and simple details make the house appear larger than it is. Atkinson and Walker went on to build one similar house, Ultuna at Oulton Broad, Suffolk.

FARNLEY HEY

Honley Road, Farnley Tyas, West Yorkshire
1953–54, 1956 and later: Peter Womersley
Listed grade II

When John Womersley married Ann Alured in October 1953 they built a house, realised in phases as building restrictions ended and their family grew. They had found the site some 18 months earlier, when Womersley's older brother Peter prepared the design. It remains the seminal mid-century modern house for its variety of materials and interlocking spaces, the English counterpart to the house Marcel Breuer built himself at Lincoln, Massachusetts, in 1938–39.

Peter Womersley (1923–93) had studied at the Architectural Association in 1947–52, winning three travel scholarships and gaining work experience in Kuwait before designing Farnley Hey. A holiday in Italy exposed him to sophisticated modern materials and the beauty of built-in fixtures. Farnley Hey is based on a timber frame, which creates a double-height main space fully glazed onto a terrace overlooking a steep drop. This is countered by an end wall of rough stone salvaged from nearby railway sidings, with other walls of pale brick, varnished shiplap timber and painted panels; the framework enabled the wing to be infilled with a garage and bedrooms later.

The interior survives little altered thanks to its long ownership by Joe Battye from 1959 to 2010. Other spaces flow out of a double-height living room designed for music and defined by a timber floor, the dining area separated by a planting trough. Stairs (the balustrade infilled with Formica in 1956) ascend to a gallery serving bedrooms and a cantilevered balcony, now glazed and infilled below.

114 KENILWORTH ROAD

Coventry
1956–57; Robert Harvey
Listed grade II

The architect Robert Harvey chose to practise in Stratford-upon-Avon while his friend Ross Harper ran the firm's main office in Birmingham. It gave him the opportunity to work for local businesses and schools and, between 1954 and 1979, to design over 30 private houses, assisted from 1961 by his wife Bet. All three had trained at the Birmingham School of Architecture, when they had discovered the work of Frank Lloyd Wright, then not well known in Britain. Wright first lectured to a packed house of students in 1939 and again in 1950, when Harvey was among the throng of admirers. They corresponded during the war, Wright touched that there was interest in his work while Britain faced its darkest hour.

Among Harvey's first houses were two for his family in the Coventry suburbs, tucked into woodland. Both are low, with big roofs and deep overhanging eaves that conceal children's bedrooms (No. 114, built for Harvey's brother, featured an attic for his three young nephews). Chains took the place of downpipes in the manner also favoured by Le Corbusier. Harvey and his family took on much of the construction work themselves, mixing simple brick with rough stone, concrete and fine timberwork within a homespun aesthetic. Harvey thought of himself as a sculptor, and every house is strongly individual. They all display great sensitivity, with here an ingenious manipulation of room heights, floor levels and interior spaces that reveal a concern for the psychological and personal sense of place so important to private houses.

ARCHITECT'S OWN HOUSE

Ingestre Road, Oxton, Merseyside
1957, 1977–78; J. Roy Parker

Joseph Parker (1926–2000, known as Jo – he considered a final 'e' irrelevant) was a characterful architect who created characterful private houses across Merseyside. He also designed restaurants and the Everyman Theatre, usually credited to the partnership Nelson & Parker, and something of the theatrical infused even his simplest buildings.

Many of his houses have been altered or demolished, but the one that Parker designed for himself and his family survives well. Its site is a shelf of land between the road and a former quarry, The Arno, where in 1957 he erected a single-storey house of brick, timber and glass. It is largely symmetrical around a central hallway, with three bedrooms on one side and an open-plan kitchen and large living area on the other. Having a budget of only about £3,500, he undertook the simpler construction work himself, but brought in expert joiners from the local shipbuilding industry for the fine detailing; with exposed roof trusses, a parquet floor and built-in furniture, timber is the dominant material. Hardwood beams supporting the roof were extended in an exaggerated manner to create a pergola, a feature that rotted and which has been removed.

Parker's later work became more eclectic – a brutalist parody of post-modernism before its time that made expressive use of sensational geometry and a strong materiality. This is seen in the additions made here in 1976, a near-pyramid over a garage with eccentric-shaped rooms and vibrant colours.

MORO HOUSE, BLACKHEATH PARK

Blackheath, London
1957–58; Peter Moro
Listed grade II*

Marcel Breuer seems to have been the first architect to set his accommodation on an upper level above such necessities as a garage and utility room.

Moro refined this reinterpretation of the *piano nobile* to give greater light and privacy to his own London home, after acquiring the substantial site from local developer Leslie Bilsby when a proposed three-storey Span terrace failed to attract buyers. The dark-painted lower floor contains a garage, guest accommodation and a substantial workshop. A broad staircase behind the main entrance separates the living and bedroom accommodation on the larger upper level. Moro then sliced the main space crosswise so that the living area and study overlooking the garden are a few steps lower than the dining area and kitchen, which permitted a clerestory to light the centre of the deep plan. It is not a large house, but in Moro's hands every element had its place, the study area (defined by the central fireplace) originally featuring built-in shelving that screened his desk, and the living space semi-fixed seating by his good friend and collaborator Robin Day.

Blackheath Park shows Moro reaching his maturity as an architect. It is cooler in design than his work at the Royal Festival Hall, using a limited palette of favourite colours – including his favourite black and white – with contrasts of dark brick, white weatherboarding, steel and tiles. The internal timber finishes and sense of calm simplicity are more reminiscent of Alvar Aalto.

HIGH SUNDERLAND

Selkirk, Borders
1957–58; Peter Womersley
Listed grade A

Bernat Klein was an émigré designer who transformed the tweed industry by introducing brilliant colours and textures. His house follows a similar discipline, substituting the warp and weft of weaving with a Miesian building grid and makore hardwood frame. He commissioned the house after he saw Farnley Hey (see page 50), also in a woollen area; Peter Womersley settled locally, building his own house and becoming a family friend. High Sunderland is unusually complex, reflecting the interplay of two strong personalities. Its aura is captured by Klein's daughter Shelley in her reminiscences, *The See-Through House*.

High Sunderland sits on a paved plinth that floats over an undisturbed landscape. Womersley controlled the design, even selecting the site, and wrote of a 'subtractive architecture, commencing with one simple volume and breaking it down'. The frame is exposed in the terraces and courtyards that separate the three interconnected sections of the single-storey house – the living area, children's rooms and a studio added in 1982. The central living area is sunken to give greater height, with a gallery on two sides and a dining area separated by a plant trough. Klein introduced maples, hardwoods and textiles to Womersley's instructions, but later substituted travertine for the floors and muted creams replaced the original fabrics of browns and reds. Womersley designed some furniture, believing that it was the only necessary ornament in a house. Klein later added the tile mosaic screen by the car port.

GIBBERD HOUSE AND GARDEN

Marsh Lane, Harlow, Essex
1957–84; (Sir) Frederick and Patricia (Lady) Gibberd
Landscape registered grade II

Writing in London, Gibberd confided to his diary in August 1951 that the only way he could stop working was to find a weekend house, 'not later than early Victorian'. Yet in January 1957 he acquired a derelict smallholding dating from 1907 on the edge of Harlow close to the River Stort. He also opened an office in the town, heading there on Fridays en route to Marsh Lane. Gibberd was refused planning permission to rebuild the house, but he made alterations and added a tall living room, with three great windows. 'I placed each for pictures of the garden, and made a garden for each of the windows,' he later explained. There was no master plan. Instead he chopped and changed his ideas over three decades, as he progressed from the garden rooms around the house to damming the Pincey Brook at the bottom of the plot for a motte and bailey castle.

Gibberd's first wife, Dorothy ('Thea'), died in 1970 and two years later Gibberd married Patricia Fox-Edwards, a charismatic local councillor who had helped to develop Harlow's remarkable sculpture collection. As a wedding present she gave him Gerda Rubinstein's *City*. There were only three sculptures in the garden then, but 80 quickly followed. The Gibberds replanned and replanted, setting some sculptures into glades, others into bases of concrete, tile and pebbles laid out by Gibberd himself, who retired there in 1978. Many of the most interesting items (like *City*) are smaller versions of works found in the town.

THE HALL, FOXES DALE

Blackheath Park, London
1958; Eric Lyons for Span Developments

Eric Lyons and Geoffrey Townsend showed that architect-designed dwellings could compete with those of developer-builders. Few others did. Meeting as students, they first realised these aims in Townsend's native Twickenham, prompting him to surrender his architect's registration to act as developer. They then took on a larger challenge, at Parkleys, Ham Common, with Lyons producing the designs. Leslie Bilsby, a builder buying up bombsites and market gardens in Blackheath Park, approached them in 1956, leading them to form Span Developments – 'span' chosen by Lyons to refer variously and obtusely to a beam or an idea.

Blackheath Park boasts the greatest concentration of Span estates of distinctive terraced houses and three-storey flats, set in huddles behind its broad Regency avenues. The earliest are light structures clad in tiles, with weatherboarding at Hallgate. Flats at The Hall and The Priory were followed in 1958 by modest two-storey terraces, after three-storey houses proved too expensive for Span's young clientele. This dainty terrace was one of the first to be built and remains the most colourful. Only in the late 1960s did larger houses prove successful, in a more muscular brick idiom.

Important to the Span 'look' is the rich planting that softens Lyons's simple structures, masterminded by Ivor Cunningham, Michael Brown and Preben Jakobsen. Geoffrey Townsend pioneered endowment mortgages and a management structure of residents' committees – a system that continues today, which along with strict covenants has ensured the survival of most Span estates as mid-century modern icons.

LASLETT HOUSE

3 Clarkson Road, Cambridge
1958; Trevor Dannatt
Listed grade II

Peter Laslett was a history professor at Cambridge and a founding force behind the Open University and the University of the Third Age. He met Dannatt through a mutual friend, Rachel Rostas. Laslett's budget and needs were modest, save that he asked for a first-floor living room to maximise the view. Dannatt had worked on the Royal Festival Hall under Peter Moro, whose own house has a similar plan to the Laslett House but one expressed in more complex elevations. Rostas had studied music in Vienna, where she had lodged with Henry Kulka, Adolf Loos's chief assistant, and the Laslett House reflects Loos's *raumplan* approach of concealing different levels in a simple rectangle, here securing a higher space for the living room by making the garage low. The clearest source, however, is a house at Vedbæk in Denmark by Erik Sørensen (himself to work in Cambridge), which Dannatt had published as editor of the *Architects' Year Book*.

The clean exterior of timber and brick conceals a complex plan, whereby the living room is set on a half-landing above the garage to give extra height. Additional interest comes from the open stairwell, which allows cross-views from the living area into the dining room in the centre of the house, where full-height windows slide fully open on to the rear garden.

Dannatt proposed an extension for the house in 1996. Following Mrs Laslett's death in 2012 the house was sold and a larger addition made by Cambridge Architectural Research Ltd.

WILSON HOUSE

16 Kevock Road, Lasswade, Midlothian
1958–59; Morris & Steedman
Listed grade B

James Morris and Robert Steedman met when students at Edinburgh College of Art. They spent a sabbatical year touring European architecture by motorbike, and in 1955 secured scholarships to the University of Pennsylvania, where Louis Kahn and Philip Johnson were among their tutors.

Morris met Mr and Mrs Wilson, a printer and his French wife looking to build a modern house, when he was researching traditional Scottish renders. They had a site on a south-facing hillside near Edinburgh, blessed with spectacular views but only 16ft (4.9m) wide. It demanded a steel frame and deep piles, resulting in a disciplined grid that determined the house's proportions, and a 4ft (1.2m) cantilever that made the site feasible. Both architects worked on the design, but Steedman completed the drawings while Morris was on National Service.

The principal rooms were set in a line overlooking the view, rather like Marcel Breuer's long, narrow houses. An external hardwood frame and white-painted brickwork gave a crisp and functional appearance. Inside, sliding doors and fold-down handles made the circulation spaces seem bigger, as did the extra height of the stair hall. A rounded end to the bathroom, responding to the shape of the tub, disrupted the view down the house, making it seem bigger. Another contrast was the fireplace in the living space, sculpted of local Craigleith stone polished smooth on the dining side, left rough and rocky facing the sitting area. The house has been extended, but the architects' key features and outdoor terraces remain.

MAMOURIAN HOUSE

Stanton, Morpeth, Northumberland
1958–59; Ryder and Yates

Alice Mamourian was from a wealthy Northumbrian land-owning family, but had lived in London for many years. On her husband's death, and in her 71st year, she sought the advice of Professor W.B. Edwards at Newcastle University on an architect to design a house on the family estate. The *Sunday Sun* reported that she sought 'an atomic cot, something concrete and modern … I have always said that I would rather have one big room than be walled up in compartments.' Edwards unhesitatingly recommended Gordon Ryder and Peter Yates, who had met working for Berthold Lubetkin at Peterlee and formed a practice in Newcastle. This was the last of a series of houses by them across Northumberland and Cumberland, though Ryder was later to design two houses for himself and his family which are among the best known of the practice's works. Most of Ryder and Yates's buildings have been demolished, and the early houses have been heavily altered.

The site was an old kitchen garden, and 18th-century bricks from its walls were incorporated into the new house. The simple rectilinear form had a single aspect and flat roof, with three large windows to the main space and a fourth to the adjoining kitchen. The narrow first-floor windows were set over small windows in the gaps between them, with a single window in the end wall. An entrance hall had its own timber box. The interior was entirely white, the main space partly subdivided by an open pine staircase and with a freestanding fireplace, a cube with a cylindrical flue.

FLATS
32 47

PARK GATE

Somerhill Road, Hove, East Sussex
1958–60; Eric Lyons and Span

Span Developments' mix of aesthetics and economics rarely stacked up commercially outside south London and Surrey. An exception was Hove, where it operated under its earlier name of Bargood Estates. Park Gate contains 47 two- and three-bedroomed flats set around landscaped courtyards, with garages tucked discreetly on one side.

Park Gate stands in the heart of Hove, where the 18th-century Wick House adjoined a popular chalybeate (iron-salts) spa, now St Ann's Wells Gardens. A scheme replacing Wick House with flats gained planning permission in 1947 but was never built. It was in February 1955 that Lyons secured outline permission for his more sensitive scheme, followed by full approval in June 1958.

The style is that of Lyons's earlier flats at Ham Common, though tile-hanging is a Sussex tradition. The difference is the height and density, for to accommodate 47 flats Park Gate has four storeys. The staircase towers are fully glazed, with coloured panes. More coloured glass conceals private stores to either side, whose open brick screens to either side provide dark contrasts as well as natural ventilation. The flats have glazed doors to the kitchens and large, open-plan living rooms. Hedges screen the ground-floor units, and larger shrubs and roses cascade over pergolas that give structure to Ivor Cunningham's dense landscaping. Windows have been altered, but Park Gate enjoys the strong community engineered by Geoffrey Townsend and Span, here with many young families.

ENTWOOD

Westwood Road, Birkenhead, Wirral
1959; Dewi-Prys Thomas
Listed grade II

Olive Banks was the daughter of an Enfield builder who lectured in sociology at Liverpool University with her husband Joe, and became a leading historian of feminism. In 1959, the year she secured a permanent post, the couple commissioned a fellow lecturer, Dewi-Prys Thomas from the School of Architecture, to build Entwood. Banks established the garden, including such distinctive 1950s species as acers, heathers and metasequoia, since 1969 lovingly maintained, along with the house, by Louis and Ursula Redington.

In 1957 Thomas had designed a house nearby, Birkenland, for another academic, Dorothea Oschinsky, taking inspiration from the site and making rigorous use of proportions like the Golden Section. Entwood followed similar principles but has a more sophisticated plan. Thomas created three pavilions that meet in the double-height dining space, truly the heart of the house. Their three monopitch gables nod in perfect harmony, their dark shapes a contrast to the Tyrolean render of the walls; now painted white, some of the details were originally blue. By pushing the bedroom wing to the rear, Thomas could light the house from the east as well as the south, and create a courtyard garden room in the angle. It was also a response to the steep site, permitting a split level to give greater height to the living room.

Dewi-Prys Thomas (1916–85) was a charismatic and inspirational lecturer, who left Liverpool in 1960 to head the Welsh School of Architecture at Cardiff University. He resumed his design career only on his retirement.

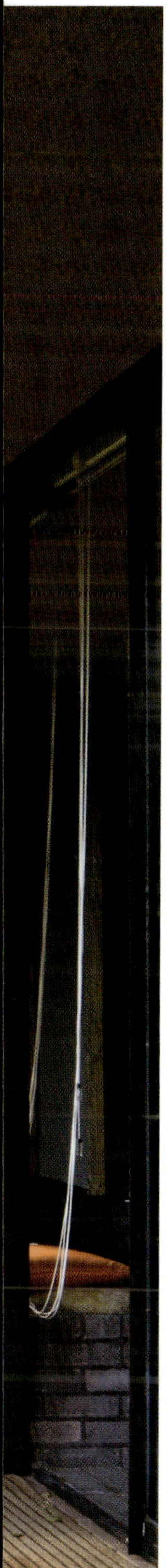

PAST FIELD

Rotherfield Road, Henley-on-Thames, Oxfordshire
1959–60, extended 1966–67; Patrick Gwynne
Listed grade II

Liz Salmon was a professional singer and pianist who worked with Geoffrey Rand, a musician and close friend of Patrick Gwynne. So when she and her husband Anthony, a Henley doctor, bought a small field on a low hill south of the town, they tentatively invited him to suggest ideas. Gwynne made a series of sketches before determining on a boomerang plan that was modern and stylish yet economical within a budget of £8,000.

The curve of the house enfolded the landscape, giving all the principal rooms long views. The roof swept upwards towards the south, where overhanging eaves gave protection from the sun in what was then a treeless foreground. A large living room, with space for two pianos, was placed in one half of the boomerang, balanced by the entrance and a line of bedrooms in the other. Hard surfaces such as exposed brickwork for the walls and floors, and a high, sloping ceiling gave excellent acoustics. Much of the furniture was built in, the main living-room sideboard supported on one of the steel poles that holds up the roof. When in 1966–67 a kitchen was added at one end of the house (the old one becoming a panelled dining room) and a master bedroom at the other, Tony Salmon did much of the joinery himself under Gwynne's exacting supervision.

In 2000 the Salmons asked Gwynne to design a new house alongside for their daughter Susie, which was realised after his death by John Allan.

CEDARWOOD

Beaconsfield Road, Woolton, Liverpool
1959–60; Gerald Beech and Dewi-Prys Thomas
Listed grade II*

California has its 'Case Study Houses', a series begun in 1945 to promote modern architecture and sell magazines, in which new houses were not only extensively published but open to visitors for a short time. British lifestyle magazines attempted similar programmes sporadically, usually in the form of a 'House of the Year'. The best known was promoted by the *Woman's Journal* in 1960, commissioned from two architects teaching at Liverpool University and seen by 50,000 people in March 1960. The journal bore the cost of the project, recouped by sponsorship from manufacturers and local retailers. Ian Mackenzie from Liverpool's premier department store, George Henry Lee, selected the internal furnishings in consultation with the architects, whose students contributed to the decoration.

Cedarwood is a house of two halves, for the upper storey is clad in the dark Canadian redwood that bequeathed its name and separated by a glazed flash gap. It masks the greater bulk of the lower floor, a wider block supporting a roof terrace and finished in contrasting white render. Inside there is cedar too, lining the walls of the open-tread staircase that is the centrepiece of the house and found in the boarded ceilings. At one end is an open living room, at the other a largely original kitchen linked by a dresser to the dining room that runs in between, with a large window overlooking the garden. Delicate detailing provides a light touch. Beech and Thomas also landscaped the rear garden, sculpting it into surprisingly large, picturesque mounds.

FIELDEND

Strawberry Hill, Twickenham, Greater London
1959–60; Eric Lyons and Span

Fieldend is more open than most other Span estates; despite being built on old gravel works and allotments, the landscaping is dominant and the housing density lower than elsewhere. It is also one of the first examples outside the new towns of an architect working with a specialist landscape consultant, here Michael Brown, one of Lyons's assistants who was also one of the first residents of Fieldend and for many years advised on its maintenance.

In 1959, the grand Victorian villas of Waldegrave Park were considered so outmoded that Geoffrey Townsend of Span easily demolished two to make an access road to his new development. The road runs in a loop around the 51 new houses, modern interpretations of Georgian terraces that face on to a staggered village green of two halves. Lyons and Ivor Cunningham had adopted a similar approach at Corner Green, Blackheath, developed two years earlier, but Fieldend is more expansive. The house types, with flat roofs and lightweight, weatherboarded facades, are also derived from those at Corner Green – the T7 and T8, where 'T' stands for terrace; they are the same 20ft (6.1m) width but the T7 is 3ft (0.91m) deeper. Lyons designed elaborate signage for all his estates, based on the Clarendon typeface, and a low, mushroom-topped aluminium light that illuminated the footpaths. It is hard to believe that none of the trees are more than 60 years old nor, conversely, that the rest of the planting layout is that old.

PARKHAM WOOD HOUSE

Parkham Road, Brixham, Devon
1960; Mervyn Seal
Listed grade II

Mervyn Seal had newly moved to Brixham to work with a local developer-builder when he was commissioned by an hotelier, John Brady, to design a house on a cliff face above the town centre. Seal was given complete freedom but little time: he produced the basic design in a day.

Parkham Wood has a broad frontage, but is only 11ft (3.4m) deep because of the cliff and a wish to maximise the fantastic views. A true cliff-hanger, it is cantilevered on a concrete slab, with brick cross-walls and timber facades; below, Seal left sections of the cliff face. He gave his sources as Frank Lloyd Wright and Le Corbusier, the eye-catching, centrally drained butterfly roof inspired by the latter's unbuilt Maison Errázuriz. The combination of such a roof with rubble stone and timber also resembles Marcel Breuer's work, the materials and topography of South Devon only a little more rugged than those of New England. Local boat builders constructed the staircases inside and out, their treads cantilevered off central spines. Le Corbusier's Unité d'Habitation inspired the large, double-height living space, which again recalls earlier examples by Breuer, particularly in the position of the master bedroom overlooking the main space. A rough limestone wall, lining the snug at one end of the living room, and boarded ceilings contrast with an original bespoke chandelier of coloured glass. This was the first of four houses with butterfly roofs built by Seal in the Torbay area and the most complete.

ENDS

KEELSON

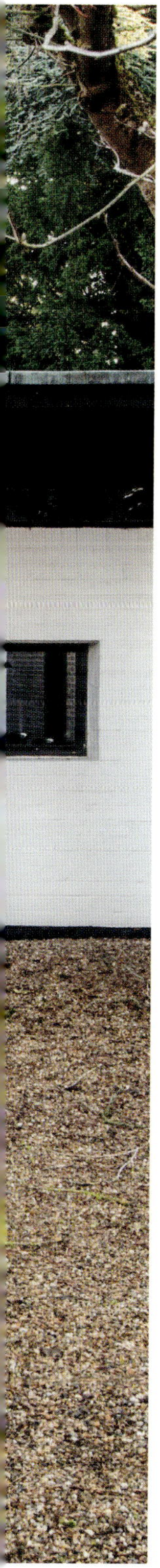

KEELSON

Hills Avenue, Cambridge
1960–61; Erik Sørensen
Listed grade II

Olga Kennard is a crystallographer and the founder of the Cambridge Structural Database. She was newly divorced with two young daughters when in 1961 she was seconded to work in Cambridge, and determined to build her own house. She found a plot, but searched across Britain in vain for an architect. She turned to her professional contacts in Denmark, whence the great physicist Niels Bohr responded, 'Sørensen and no one else!' Although Scandinavian influences were strong in post-war architecture, few foreign architects actually built in Britain then. Dr Kennard remains delighted with her decision.

The understated elegance of Keelson (the name comes from timber ship construction) owes much to its wooden frame, which is infilled with white-painted brickwork to a carefully irregular pattern to the front and large areas of glass to the rear. Sørensen made best use of the narrow site for the 'U'-shaped, single-storey house. The entrance, dining room and kitchen fills the width at the front, whence a long gallery lined with books leads past small bedrooms for the children and a live-in nanny, now adapted as a master bedroom, to an open living area at the rear (now extended into the former bedroom and study area there). It encloses a courtyard, with a larger lawn to the rear. Sørensen also selected some of the Danish furniture.

Kennard also commissioned Sørensen to design Cambridge's Crystallographic Data Centre in 1990–92 and as a trustee of the British Museum advised on its extension by Rogers Stirk Harbour in 2014.

BEECHWORTH CLOSE

Hampstead Heath, London
1960–61; Patrick Gwynne
Listed grade II

Max and Anne Bruh, German refugees who met and married in London, revived the defunct Frank Usher fashion label to specialise in dress design. With growing sons, they bought a plot on the south side of Hampstead Heath and sought a house that was easy to run, 'with a certain toughness to withstand the mild ravages which even the nicest teenagers are liable to perpetrate', as they told *Home* magazine. When they struggled to find an architect, a friend recommended they visit a nearby house, The Firs, the first major post-war work by Patrick Gwynne, a lover of witty, elegant design, hard finishes and built-in furniture.

The Bruhs's budget was generous – there is even a string of servants' bells in the kitchen, which has its own entrance. The scale was sufficiently large for Gwynne to set back the upper storey, emphasised by contrasting grey-black bricks and white render within a concrete frame finished in black 'Glamorock'. The authorship of the semi-abstract relief is unknown. Gwynne made a feature of centrally planned, top-lit staircases, here continuing the theme of the exterior with white terrazzo and black mosaic, contrasted with timber panelling. The garden lies to the north, but Gwynne gave the large living room a double aspect so it also has sunshine. At his suggestion, the black lacquered sideboard was given gold Chinese decoration by the artist Peter Thompson, an oriental refrain developed in the living room with red silk seat coverings and buff silk wallpaper. Gwynne even advised on the garden planting.

HUNT AND STEEDMAN HOUSES

Ravelston Dykes Road, Edinburgh
1960–62; Morris & Steedman
Listed grade B

With two small children (a third was born in 1962), Robert Steedman looked to build himself a house. A local builder offered land on condition that Steedman secured permission for two houses and that he could erect them. Set behind a Victorian lodge and walls in a green lung between school playing fields and two golf courses, the linked pair of houses were white and modern yet complemented their setting. They were almost identical in appearance and plan, but Steedman stepped them down the slope to give greater privacy and some asymmetry, with a set-in car port and roof terrace to give further articulation.

The site was shielded by trees, and to maximise the light and views Steedman placed the living rooms on the upper floors, reached by circular stairs that opened into a main space looking west with a dining alcove facing east. Continuous frameless sliding windows and a built-in window seat accentuate the chic simplicity of this living area, along with timber wall linings and ceilings. The roof was supported on glulam beams, one with a sliding screen that could be pulled across to make a cosy snug. A kitchen and laundry are concealed off the dining area. The two houses shared the rear garden, with few flowers to disturb the greensward. Steedman recalled that 'it was a thrilling experience to live in a modern house for the first time, with flexibility to move furniture, though you settle down to a similar pattern'. It is little altered.

SPENCE HOUSE

Beaulieu, Hampshire
1961; Sir Basil Spence
Listed grade II

At the height of his fame, as he was completing Coventry Cathedral, extending Southampton University and designing a new campus in Sussex, Spence built himself a holiday home. He enjoyed long weekends away from his home-cum-office in Canonbury, and on the Beaulieu River near Southampton he combined intense days of drawing with a passion for sailing.

The brick ground floor was originally designed as a storage space for Spence's yacht, a workroom and a changing area. The living accommodation was on the upper floor, formed of concrete and cedar boarding, with a deep cantilevered balcony overlooking the river separated by a giant sliding window from a large open-plan living area, a galley kitchen, and cabin-like bedrooms and bathrooms. The dominating feature is a gigantic concrete fireplace designed by Spence, engineered by Ove Arup and bushhammered by a machine quietly 'vacationed' from Coventry Cathedral. Otherwise the matchboard finishes give the sense of being aboard a uniquely comfortable English wherry. In the woods he built a separate studio.

By 1962 Spence had converted the ground floor into a kitchen and dining room. He added a stair tower to the east side connecting the two floors, glazed the balcony to extend the living area and extended the studio, yet retained the ethos of a mudlarking weekend. Spence had no help from his huge office and the showmanship added to the simple design is all his own. Renovations and additions by John Purdey in 1998–2001 have been extensive but sympathetic.

PALAFITTE

Woodlands Road, Bushey, Hertfordshire
1961–62; John Prizeman

Mr and Mrs Buttle wanted a house for themselves and two teenage children that would also serve them through their retirement. The *Weekend Review* in March 1962 called Prizeman's solution 'an idea to fit a family, to-day and years ahead'. It worked – Palafitte survives so perfectly because it was lived in by Mrs Buttle into the 2000s, and has since been beautifully restored. The name Palafitte references a small, single-storey Neolithic and Bronze Age house found on lakeshores and marshes across western Europe, which comprised a wooden platform supported on poles driven into the ground. Here is a thoroughly modern timber house, but one raised on steel poles at the corners, as is the projecting sundeck over the central garage – which has the only solid supporting walls.

The other walls are of timber, inside and out, with exposed joists to the slightly dished 'butterfly' roof. The first floor, mainly of western red cedar and Pacific Coast hemlock, contains all the living accommodation. The living areas are to the front, with four bedrooms to the rear and a central line of services in a deceptively deep plan. There are six large windows to the front: two in each end bay are set either side of sliding windows leading on to the sundeck. Either side of the garage is covered parking, with to the left a fully glazed hallway featuring a bold dog-leg stair. John Prizeman (1930–92) designed a number of similar houses, but this is the lone survivor in original condition.

GRANGE ESTATE

Castlebar Hill, Ealing, London
1963–66, 1972–74; Kenneth Bland for Wates Estates

Ealing was 'the queen of the suburbs' in late Victorian times, when substantial villas were erected on the rising ground of Castlebar Hill, north of the old town. One of them, The Grange, itself replaced an earlier house, Castlebar Park, from which only a fishpond and some trees survive.

Wates, a major south London building firm with its own architect, Kenneth Bland (1909–83), rivalled Span Developments in building carefully designed and landscaped housing at moderate cost. Bland had a long career with Wates from 1933 until the 1970s, also designing Mulberry harbours during the Second World War. This is his masterpiece. He ringed the existing pond and trees with three-storey flats and houses, which repeat the bands of glazing and tile-hanging made fashionable for modern housing by Eric Lyons and Span. More houses are set in culs-de-sac, some with pronounced zigzags of linked pitched roofs. At the estate's centre is a single ten-storey point block, The Cedars, its broken 'T'-shaped form responding to the shape of the surrounding pine trees. A second block, The Grange, was added nearly a decade later using the same brick to give coherence.

The landscaping is particularly careful, designed by Derek Lovejoy & Associates, who were Wates's regular landscape architects. It is artfully natural around the pond, with an open greensward that enhances the Victorian planting. Elsewhere are broad terraces on several levels, paved with cobbles and lined with circular planters. Lovejoy's firm itself turned to designing housing at Wates's adjoining White Ledges estate of 1968.

ANSTY PLUM

Ansty, Wiltshire
1964; David Levitt

Roger Rigby (1922–2019) was Ove Arup's administrative partner, friend to many architects and engineers. Following the birth of their second child in 1962, he and his wife Patricia began looking for a weekend house. A friend, Sam Graves, drew their attention to a site in Ansty where a former gardener, Victor Tucker, had abandoned building a bungalow. Rigby wanted a simple house arranged around a raised hearth and sleeping gallery, inspired by the work of another friend, Edward Samuel. Philip Dowson suggested a big overhanging roof to obviate gutters and make a small house seem bigger, but he was then setting up Arup Associates and had no time to make the design; he recommended a young newcomer to the Arup office, David Levitt, later to make a reputation designing social housing. Levitt used the steeply sloping site to create a little house on two levels under a big open roof of Douglas fir, all for £4,200. The fragments of Tucker's bungalow became an enclosed garden halfway down the site.

Ove Arup introduced Rigby to Peter Smithson, who also had a weekend cottage nearby. He added a garage and studio at the bottom of the site in 1971–72, using stone and concrete to create a pocket brutalist battleship which he called 'Fort Rigby'. In 1986–87 he and Alison Smithson added the curve of steps to the main house. Sandra Coppin of Coppin Dockray Architects bought Ansty Plum with her husband Nico de Beer in 2009 and slowly restored the two elements, respecting and enhancing their different aesthetics.

HIGH BANK

Mill Hill Lane, Brockham, Surrey
1966–67; John and Beryl Higgins

John Higgins and Beryl Cook met working at the London County Council, joining the Architect's Department General Division in 1953, where they specialised in designing old people's homes. They married in 1957 and moved to Little Bookham, Surrey, where the first of three sons was born in 1959. It was in 1963 that they found a narrow half-acre plot to build their own house at Brockham, near Dorking, after John had obtained a second qualification in landscape architecture.

The site was a tangle of brambles, with some mature trees and a derelict bungalow, in which the family lived while building their new house. They produced a modern design, but assumed that the district council would demand it be toned down; they were surprised and delighted when the plans were passed first time. Beryl Higgins acknowledged Frank Lloyd Wright's Fallingwater as a source. To enjoy the view to the south, they placed the living room on the first floor, reached by an open stair, with built-in furniture, beech floor and special shelving for plants. The upper storey appears to float on its cantilevered steel frame over a smaller ground floor separated by clerestory glazing. Other windows stretch from floor to ceiling to maximise the light; the sheltered ground-floor windows and sliding doors are the original Crittall steel units. A driveway through the ground floor links the garden front and back, and an outdoor stair from a first-floor balcony connects the living room to the generous garden.

Chert

CHERT

Castle Court, St Lawrence, Ventnor, Isle of Wight
1967–70; Haddock and McDowell with Gilbert and Hobson of Ventnor

Koo Haddock was an engineer and Connie McDowell a scientist and factory inspector. They mustered their technical expertise to design a house for their retirement after visiting the New York World's Fair in 1964, employing local architects to work up their design. Named after a type of flint and built of concrete, brick, wood and glass, Chert nestles in an avenue of 1960s villas lined up against the cliff facing the sea. The ground floor has garaging and a workshop where Miss Haddock set pebble patterns into slabs of concrete that decorate the house and garden. The principal rooms are on the first floor behind a large balcony overlooking the sea.

Chert's facade gives more clues to the house's plan. In the centre is a glazed entrance and a spiral staircase that leads to the main rooms. Either side, symmetrically arranged, are a garage, a near-identical kitchen and bathroom – still fitted in turquoise Formica and turquoise and orange tiles – as well as two reception rooms that could be thrown together by means of large folding doors. There were originally no bedrooms, just day beds. Haddock and McDowell added the single-storey Little Chert to the side as detached accommodation for their visitors and created two small pools.

On their deaths, the ladies bequeathed the house to the National Trust, who recognised that people might want to holiday in a mid-century house. It introduced more conventional sleeping arrangements for its guests on opening in 2000 but otherwise left it little altered.

LOW-COST HOUSING

PERSANT ROAD

Excalibur Estate, Catford, London
1945–46; R.G. Booth, Uni-Seco Structures Ltd
Nos.1–7 (odd numbers), 25 and 39 listed grade II

Rather more of Persant Road survives than the six listed houses, just about enough to give a sense of what was once London's largest 'prefab' estate with 187 houses and even a prefabricated church (St Mark's). The land was intended as an open space but London was desperate for housing in 1945, so was laid out with streets named after the Knights of the Round Table – hence the estate's name. Prisoners of war helped lay the concrete foundation slabs. Estates in Great Yarmouth and Newport (Wales) were larger, but have been demolished.

Prefabs were planned as temporary houses to be erected quickly after the war, with Winston Churchill promising up to half a million. The relatively high cost of construction meant, however, that only 156,323 were erected to 11 approved types, though thousands lasted far longer than the 10 to 15 years originally intended. The most popular types were exhibited at the Tate Gallery in late 1944. They included the Uni-Seco, the most modern-looking design, which dominated in the South East. Booth's design featured asbestos cement sheeting on a timber frame with a near-flat roof, with either a corner entrance (Mark 2) or a more practical central door (Mark 3). Both versions survive on Persant Road.

Prefabs were popular, boasting fitted kitchens and bathrooms, and built-in shelves and cupboards, since furniture was in short supply. They became ideal bungalows for the elderly or people with physical disabilities, and the Excalibur Estate was a proud, close-knit community until it was swept away in the 2010s.

SWEDISH PREFABS

Marshland St James, near Wisbech, Norfolk
c. 1946; Arthur Kenyon and Robert Matthew with Svenska Trähus

One of the most curious products of the wartime fascination with prefabricated housing was a programme of timber houses from Sweden. Companies there began producing flat-packed housing in the late 19th century for emigrants to take to the United States. In 1943 Cyril Sjöström, an Anglo-Finnish architect with Swedish ancestry who adopted his mother's name of Mardall when he joined F.R.S. Yorke in partnership, worked with MI6 to bring Swedish prefabs to Britain, only for the Nazis to intercept them. The English architects Arthur Kenyon and Robert Matthew then produced a design that was manufactured in Sweden for the British Government. Only 5,000 pairs were imported because of currency restrictions that saw softwood in short supply until the early 1950s.

There were four designs, two of which were intended for England and Wales and two for Scotland. Marshland St James, a linear settlement that began to grow in the 1920s, has both the two-storey semi-detached 'Type A' variety with a projecting washhouse, and a smaller 'Type D' version with the upper storey set in the roof. Scotland also saw pairs without the washhouses and a four-unit terraced version. All have solid sections of vertical matchboarding. The first pairs were erected in Abbots Langley, Hertfordshire and Tannochside, Lanarkshire, in 1945. The English versions were all intended for rural areas, and can be found most extensively across East Anglia, around Doncaster (where a pair of Type D houses are listed) and in Gloucestershire. The programme was abandoned in 1948.

GAER
STELVIO ESTATE

Newport

1946–51; Johnson Blackett, borough architect

Johnson Blackett (1896–1984) was a self-confessed modernist who had travelled widely in Europe after completing his architectural training at Liverpool University. He was one of the first of its prestigious graduates to make a career as a borough architect when in 1925 he accepted a post as deputy at Newport, Gwent. The Liverpool School of Architecture dominated local authority departments after 1945. Here the job architect was his assistant Alfred Williams, and the result was remarkably ambitious for its date.

Gaer is a series of 25 curved terraces all named after English or Scottish writers, on a big, open hillside beneath the Tredegar hill fort. The terraces, with their contrasts of brick and render under near-flat roofs, wend their way in curves, gently twisting inside and out along the contours – only one side of each cul-de-sac is built on. The longest terraces, on Dickens Drive, are at the bottom of the slope. At the top are three-storey flats, off Shakespeare Crescent, where full-height stair windows and flanking balconies, concrete porch roofs and single-storey brick storage blocks are linked together in a skilful composition. One of Britain's largest prefab estates sat on the adjoining slopes until the late 2000s.

Attached to the houses is a perky primary school, also begun in 1949 (listed grade II), of brown brick with porthole windows and a square clock tower from which long fingers of classrooms radiate under projecting eaves. It boldly sports the scheme's Festival of Britain plaque, the only one awarded to Wales.

HALLFIELD ESTATE

Paddington, London
1947–54; by Drake and Lasdun in succession to Tecton
Listed grade II

The rich had long fled Paddington's stuccoed terraces, and they were already run-down and sub-divided when bombing inflicted a coup de grâce. Today new and old blocks sparkle side by side. Hallfield was an ambitious early piece of post-war rebuilding, secured for Tecton by its youngest partner Denys Lasdun and taken over by him when Berthold Lubetkin dissolved the practice in 1948.

Hallfield was to have been even larger than was realised. Lubetkin bequeathed a layout of ten-storey blocks facing east–west and six-storey blocks running north–south, between which he planned to continue the adjoining road as a loop rather than create a separate estate road. Today, the separation of the estate, set below the rising ground of Bishops Bridge Road in a sea of grass and mature trees, contributes to its charm. Otherwise the blocks would be more imposing on the surrounding terraces. The concrete balcony fronts make giant patterns against the dark-red brickwork of the flats and the tiles of their surrounding framework and kinked access steps – harsher now the concrete panels have been painted. Balconies on the smaller blocks resemble giant sledges hoisted into the sky. All Tecton's post-war flats have chequerboard facades, inspired by the patterned *kelims* of Lubetkin's native Caucasia, but these are the most dramatic. Note, too, the freestanding 1950s concrete signboards directing visitors round the estate. Lasdun added The Forum, a block of communal facilities and pensioners' flats, and Hallfield School (grade II*).

CHURCHILL GARDENS

Pimlico, Westminster, London
1947–62; Powell & Moya
First phase, plus Gilbert and Sullivan Houses, listed grade II

In 1943, the government asked London's boroughs to produce housing plans for implementation immediately hostilities ended. Westminster identified an exceptionally large site, and in 1945 held a competition, won by Philip Powell and Hidalgo Moya, both then only in their mid-twenties. They proposed tall blocks at right angles to the river and a winding estate road, with lower ranges (including houses) parallel to them. The initial four ten-storey blocks, named after poets, were inspired by the Bergpolder flats in Rotterdam (which they had just visited) and Lubetkin's 'working-class flats' project of 1935. Glazed staircases and round lift tops punctuate the long facades, in a setting of lawns and shrubs. Completed in 1951, this was the first development with a district heating system, fed by waste heat from Battersea Power Station piped into a glazed accumulator tower.

Smaller flats followed at the western end of the site, beginning with Gilbert House and Sullivan House, which set the style of the later blocks with glass dominating the facades. A Victorian school and public house were retained, and a community centre and open square added late to the plan. The final phase was completely different – a lower, snake-like block on the eastern edge of the estate that shields it from the outside world. Powell and Moya lined Lupus Street with shops and a public house, and here and to the immediate south-east are blocks of maisonettes, still a novelty in the early 1950s. As impressive is the landscaping of informal squares, shielded by low rails; Powell's playgrounds, featuring a real steamroller, have gone.

THE LAWN

Mark Hall Moors, Harlow, Essex
1950–51; Frederick Gibberd
Listed grade II

Frederick Gibberd produced a master plan for the new town of Harlow in 1947–48 and served as its consultant architect for 35 years. No other architect had such authority over a town, which still reflects his interests in art and landscape as well as planning, well seen in the first and most picturesque neighbourhood, Mark Hall North, based around a Victorian estate immediately west of the old market town.

Gibberd believed in 'mixed development', that a variety of flats and houses designed for all ages and family sizes made the best use of England's limited supply of land and looked more interesting than swathes of one or the other. Aimed at young single people and couples, the ten-storey Lawn was Britain's first point block, the term derived from the Swedish *punkthus*. Gibberd justified the expense by seeking to preserve a group of oak trees, though its real importance was as a visual contrast to the surrounding houses and three-storey flats. He wrote of the importance of designing for the moving eye, choosing bold and simple scenic effects for the car driver, 'where the tall block will suddenly come into view in a gap in the development and will as suddenly fade away'. The Lawn's unique butterfly plan gave all four flats on each floor south-facing living rooms and balconies, while its elevations contrast areas of Scandinavian patterned brickwork with blue tiles and render. Lack of demand for flats ensured no more towers were built in new towns until the late 1950s.

LODDON NEW TOWN

Hobart Road, Loddon, Norfolk
1952–53; Tayler & Green

Piped water, mains electricity and sewers were still rare in rural England in 1945, when better housing was recognised as important to keep farm workers on the land. The problem was grasped by Loddon Rural District Council and their consultant architects. David Green had returned to nearby Lowestoft to run his father's practice, having met Herbert Tayler while studying at the Architectural Association.

Tayler was the designer, Green the committee man and service engineer. Ernst May's Frankfurt housing inspired the first long terraces at Ditchingham, preferred to the conventional council-house 'semi' because they respected the long lines of the open landscape. As only poor Fletton bricks were available the houses were colour-washed in pinks, blues and creams, a local tradition like the pantiled roofs.

Council bungalows for pensioners were a post-war innovation, which Tayler began designing in terraces as early as 1948. Rows are linked by crinkle-crankle walls, traditional double-curved walls for protecting fruit trees used here to conceal scruffy back gardens. As better bricks became available around 1951, Tayler and Green began to exploit their contrasting colours in intricate patterns, including projecting bricks and dates in the gables, contrasted with delicate trellises and porches. These ideas came together in their largest scheme, an extension to the market town that they dubbed 'Loddon New Town'. Tayler regretted not being able to build a pub or shops, and a scheme for council offices was never realised; they did, however, design 709 housing units for the council between 1945 and 1973.

BEVIN COURT

Cruikshank Street, Islington, London
1952–54; Skinner, Bailey & Lubetkin
Listed grade II*

Berthold Lubetkin's last and most idiosyncratic scheme for Finsbury Borough Council followed the bombing of Holford Square. Lenin had stayed there in 1902–03 and in 1942 it seemed appropriate to commemorate Britain's alliance with the Soviet Union. But a monument erected there was repeatedly vandalised and quietly removed; it is now in the Islington Museum. The replacement flats were named after Britain's first foreign secretary of the Cold War, Ernest Bevin.

Lubetkin first proposed a series of staggered replacement blocks in the form of a square. But the London County Council wanted the west side left open as a playground, and he was unwilling to erect north-facing flats. He recommended a single large block, and to ensure a sunny aspect for all the flats and a minimum of overlooking, chose a 'Y' shape. This was perfect too for Lubetkin's love of patterned surfaces. Alternating floor plans were expressed externally in a chequered pattern of brick and concrete panels faced with Hopton Wood chippings, now painted white. A four-storey block, Holford House, forms a punctuation point on Percy Circus.

Nothing prepares you for the dramatic staircase in the internal drum where the arms of the 'Y' meet. Lubetkin's conceit was to suspend half-landings between the floors at the centre of the space. Each flight goes first into the middle and then out at an angle to the galleries, where the pedestrian has to make a quarter-turn before ascending the next landing. 'A staircase is a dance,' Lubetkin claimed. His assistant Peter Yates painted a mural at the entrance.

ALTON EAST

Bessborough Road, Roehampton, London
1952–55; London County Council Architect's Department
Point blocks listed grade II

Over 70,000 buildings in the old county of London were destroyed in the Second World War, and another 1.7 million badly damaged. The London County Council had been a force in public housing in the 1890s, but such was the pressure in 1945 on rapid results over design that it passed the task to its valuation department. When the architects resumed command in 1950 they looked to revive their forebears' pioneering spirit. The team included Oliver Cox and Graeme Shankland, who had visited Sweden (see Templewood School, page 130).

Within the London boundary the chief substantial housing sites were at Roehampton, a mix of large 1850s villas and 18th-century estates. The team assigned to Portsmouth Road under the leadership of Rosemary Stjernstedt, recruited from Stevenage, sought a personal touch through detailing, landscaping and colour. Cox had seen the ten-storey point blocks built to a square plan with internal bathrooms by Backström & Reinius at Danviksklippan, Stockholm, and he developed a lighter, more sophisticated version at what became Alton East. These the team set on the sites of the Victorian villas to retain the surrounding planting, and placed houses and four-storey terraces of maisonettes on the slopes below. The preserved Victorian conifers and some scattered rocks combined with contrasting red and white bricks and coloured tiles to give an authentic Scandinavian feel while providing a truly British mixed development of various housing types.

GOLDEN LANE ESTATE

Goswell Road, City of London
1953–63; Chamberlin, Powell and Bon
Listed grade II (Crescent House II*)

Visitors to the Barbican may never notice the little estate of yellow, red and blue blocks immediately to its north, let alone realise that it was by the same architects. The City Corporation held a competition in 1951–52. Chamberlin, Powell and Bon submitted separate entries to increase their chances of winning; when Geoffry Powell triumphed, they formed a partnership.

Powell turned the estate inwards so residents did not have to overlook the acres of surrounding bombsites. 'There is no attempt at the informal in these courts,' Powell explained in 1957 of the difference between most 1950s housing and Golden Lane's grid-like plan, set on a series of levels. Deep basements left by bombed warehousing were exploited to make sunken gardens (featuring a circular stone bastion) and tennis courts, and other features include a sports centre, playground, community centre and tenants' hall. To achieve the maximum permitted density, two-bedroom maisonettes were placed around a tower of smaller flats, which at 16 storeys was briefly the tallest in Britain. It stands out for its aluminium and golden glass cladding, and a flying concrete roof that screens a water tank. A roof garden (closed in 1981) features a pool and pergola. More small flats were added when the site was extended westwards to Goswell Road in 1957. Crescent House, hugging the curve of the road with shops and a pub, introduced a tougher aesthetic of pick-marked concrete and dark timber, anticipating the style of the adjoining Barbican development where CPB were then producing the final design.

GLEADLESS VALLEY

Sheffield

1955–62; Sheffield City Architect's Department under J.L. Womersley

A steep-sided valley with a north-facing slope was a difficult place to build housing, and a controversial use of a beauty spot popular with ramblers. But Sheffield was acutely short of land for housing, and Gleadless offered accommodation for 17,000 people in a virtual new town. The difficulty for the architects – D.R. Paxton, A.N. Tunley, G.M.D. Elson, J. Gray and G.A. Butcher – was the slope, for half the land had an incline greater than one in eight. They preserved the valley bottom of the Meers Brook and The Lumb as Rollestone Wood, interspersed with playing fields, while the slightly flatter upper parts were developed in three distinct neighbourhoods, Rollestone, Hemsworth and Herdings, separated by further woodland.

Three tower blocks marked the highest point of the valley at Herdings, now reduced to two because of subsidence; these have been overclad. Following the principle of 'mixed development', the architects produced distinctive terraced houses 'along the contours' to exploit the slope, with living rooms on the upper levels to exploit the views, contrasted with narrower terraces 'across the contours', their pathways angled to minimise gradients for prams. Most distinctive are the flats set off Blackstock Road, where six-storey maisonettes are entered at mid-level so there is no need for lifts. They leave the land open for magnificent views across the valley to Donald Martin-Smith's Holy Cross Church, added as an eye-catcher in 1964–65 and whose soaring roof sweeps high above surrounding housing kept deliberately low.

EDUCATION

BUSES ONLY

GROPIUS BUILDING

Impington Village College, Impington, Cambridgeshire
1938–39; Walter Gropius and E. Maxwell Fry with Jack Howe
Listed grade I

The highest listing grade denotes the importance of this building to post-war architecture; the architecture is modest, but its social aims and influences were enormous.

Henry Morris, education officer for Cambridgeshire County Council, thought that good community facilities in rural schools might reduce the exodus from the land, still a major issue in the 1930s. Between 1927 and 1938 he built 'village colleges' at Sawston, Linton and Bottisham, in a variety of styles by successive county architects. Impington offered the same ingredients – a well-equipped school with a large hall that could be used for film shows and amateur dramatics, and in front an 'adult wing' denoted by a gentle curve and containing a library, billiards hall and meeting rooms. But Impington was the most ambitious, for Morris secured private finance to bring in a world-renowned architect and teacher that gave his project lasting fame. Even so, the original design had to be reduced to meet its modest budget and most of the final design was by Fry and Howe. Gropius had already established the style, however, and it was not that of international modernism but understated and user-friendly, using local bricks and blue tiles as well as large areas of glass. The main spaces are the large hall and a broad concourse for exhibitions and socialising. It anticipated the informal, child-friendly idiom adopted by local authorities after 1945. Morris's ideas were adopted elsewhere, but remain strongest in Cambridgeshire, where the most recent village college opened at Cambourne in 2013.

HATFIELD TECHNICAL COLLEGE / UNIVERSITY OF HERTFORDSHIRE

Hatfield, Hertfordshire
1948–52; Howard Robertson of Easton & Robertson

Hatfield was the first technical college built after the war, on land donated by the nearby de Havilland aircraft works. Originally offering secretarial as well as scientific courses, it was designated a polytechnic in 1969 and became a university in 1992. The main block is a large hall with a refectory underneath, separated from the classrooms so it could be used independently. Most of the lower ranges were prefabricated in concrete by the engineer Felix Samuely, and faced in cedar shingles because bricks were unobtainable. The tall glazed gable owes much to C.F. Møller's Aarhus University, Denmark, built from 1931 in a similar blond brick to that used here when supplies became available. Robertson varied the brick bonds to give more decoration, though the many gables and projections give the facades a spirited mid-century busyness that shines through later alterations. A technical school for 13–15-year-olds (now the Hutton Hub) was added in 1953, linked by set-back classroom ranges.

A marble relief by Trevor Tennant depicting the plan has been moved from the original first-floor entrance to a new lobby created in 2014 by Vincent & Gorbing at the other end of the block. Such was the college's importance that Hertfordshire County Council also commissioned a relief from Barbara Hepworth, *Vertical Forms* (1951): three linked figures in Hopton stone fixed on the corner of the main building. In 2019 it was removed for conservation and relocated indoors along with contemporary works commissioned from Ben Nicholson and Reg Butler.

TEMPLEWOOD SCHOOL

Pentley Park Road, Welwyn Garden City, Hertfordshire
1949–50; A.W. Cleeve Barr, Hertfordshire County Council
Listed grade II*

Hertfordshire received many evacuees from London during the Second World War, who settled on new estates and in new towns like Welwyn, and its architect's department recognised that it needed ten primary schools a year to meet rising birth rates. The deputy architect, Stirrat Johnson-Marshall, revived wartime strategies, turning to steel-framed huts developed by Hills of West Bromwich, which he and his idealistic young assistants adapted into a flexible system for building schools to any shape and size. Every detail was considered from a child's perspective, so the windows were low, sinks and lavatories small, and informal tables preferred to desks. Corridors were painted in bright colours, with more muted shades for classrooms.

Cheshunt was the first school. In the infants, by Mary Crowley, Hills's structural 8ft 3in (2.5m) grid is clearly seen in the projecting classrooms and linked cloakrooms. At Essendon, a sculpture by Georg Ehrlich launched an art programme. The most interesting schools were in the next annual batches, including Templewood, where staggered classrooms permitted more windows at a time of concern for children's eyesight and vertical cladding aided flexibility. Templewood has a fine woodland setting and unusual panache. It also has three murals by Pat Tew in the entrance area and dining hall, depicting scenes from Russian folktales, combining the romanticism and radical socialism behind many of these architects and artists. The Hertfordshire schools programme was the chief instance of prefabrication proving successful on every social and architectural level.

BRANDLEHOW SCHOOL AND GREENSIDE SCHOOL

Putney and Hammersmith, London
1950–52; Ernö Goldfinger
Brandlehow listed grade II, Greenside listed grade II*

The London County Council commissioned Goldfinger to adapt standard Ministry of Education huts into replacement buildings for Westville Road (now Greenside) and Brandlehow schools, destroyed in the Second World War. Instead he proposed his own system of prefabricated concrete trusses and beams, which saved on steel and were cheap and quick to build. While still referred to as 'huts' to secure government funding, Goldfinger's design offered better-sized rooms, corridors, natural lighting and ventilation, and he introduced decent central heating and reliable hot water. The external cladding was a cavity-wall construction with facing bricks on the outside and rendered tiles within. The headmistress at Brandlehow admired the 'chapel quality' of her school's red bricks; Westville Road (opened in 1951) got regular yellow stocks. The cost was estimated at no more than the huts, save for the higher and better-proportioned assembly hall. Brandlehow was delayed because of a shortage of steel windows thanks to the Korean War and was opened by the popular broadcaster Wilfred Pickles only in June 1952. Both schools have been sympathetically extended, Brandlehow including a classroom by Goldfinger from the 1960s.

Westville Road features a remarkable mural by Gordon Cullen created in 1952–53, featuring cameos of nature scenes, boats and the Comet aircraft, based on themes suggested by Goldfinger. He proposed that F.H.K. Henrion paint a mural at Brandlehow, but the LCC refused to pay the £200 fee.

WEST BUILDING AND APPLEBEY THEATRE

Durham University, Durham

1950–52; J.S. Allen and William Whitfield

'The design was evolved to create a series of contrasts and spatial interplays; in places, even abrupt shocks.' So claimed *Building* magazine in October 1952 with some justification. There is stone to the entrance, copper to the roofs and window surrounds, projecting balconies, and a large semi-detached lecture theatre tucked down the slope has the shape of an animal all its own. Inside, chandeliers came from Glamis Castle, to which the Bowes-Lyon family had transferred the contents of Gibside Hall, Durham.

Joseph Allen was Durham University's first head of town and country planning, appointed in 1946 having earlier set up a course in Leeds. As well as organising the first full-time planning course at its Newcastle campus (later Newcastle University), he was also charged to produce a master plan for the development of the main Durham University site south of the city's historic peninsula. The new halls of residence were classical, referencing local traditions, but the teaching buildings were modern. Only Nottingham University, also expanding rapidly, made a similar stylistic split. The West Building, for the geography and mathematics departments, was the first teaching building, attributed to Allen but actually by his brilliant assistant and a graduate of the university's School of Architecture, William Whitfield. It was the first building by an architect whose long career saw him move through brutalism to post-modernism, in part directed by the use of both styles in intelligent extensions to historic buildings, where 'contrasts and spatial interplays' became the one regular feature of his work.

YMCA INDIAN STUDENT HOSTEL

Fitzroy Square, Camden, London
1950–52, 1962–64; Ralph Tubbs
Listed grade II

This hostel is a gallant symbol of a newly independent nation, built as a base for Indian students in London. It replaced a hostel founded in 1920 by K.T. Paul, which in 1923 moved to permanent premises in Gower Street; it was acquired by University College after wartime bombing in return for this site. Money from the War Damage Commission made possible this deceptively complex replacement.

'I do not want my house to be walled on all sides nor my windows to be shut. I want the culture of all lands to blow about my house as freely as possible.' This quotation from Mahatma Gandhi was inscribed on the foundation stone.

Tubbs was anxious to avoid parallel lines where possible – hence the main stair's acute angles and raking rear windows that also give interest to the internal spaces. The building has a close relationship with Fitzroy Square, where Robert Adam's two terraces governed its height and massing, but not its style. Tubbs was the architect of the Festival of Britain's Dome of Discovery, and here he created a striking brick facade with a mix of long strip windows and smaller openings all framed in a stone surround that continues as the side walls. The large first-floor windows light reading and television rooms, while a rooftop non-denominational prayer room gives weight to the corner of the square. The basement hall has been used for high-profile cultural and political events. Tubbs extended the block in 1960–62, and more additions were made in 2002–04.

INDIAN YMCA
INDIAN YMCA

ADEMY

KIDBROOKE SCHOOL / HALLEY ACADEMY

Corelli Road, Kidbrooke, London
1951–54; Charles Pike of Slater, Moberly, Uren and Pike
Listed grade II

This was the first comprehensive school in London and one of the first in England. It was designed for 2,000 girls, and Pike's challenge was to design a hall large enough to hold them all, while making the building feel friendly at a time when such a large school was almost unique. This was done using colour, a variety of materials, quirky details and curved as well as rectangular shapes. There were originally 36 classrooms, set in three three-storey ranges around a central library and staffroom, and no fewer than five gymnasia. The largest classrooms could be divided by folding partitions when necessary and doubled up as dining rooms.

For the hall, Ove Arup and Partners engineered a shell concrete dome only three inches thick, post-tensioned using the Freyssinet system and clad in copper. For the rest, Pike combined warm Leicestershire brick with Canadian shingles and blue tiles. The other prominent feature is the clock over the entrance – just 12 round numbers and a pair of hands. More Scandinavian detailing is found elsewhere in the building, as in the double-height entrance hall with its circular skylights and a beautiful elliptical room on the roof intended as a painting studio. Many interiors feature a playful elongated diamond motif, seen in fixed benches and shelving, the stair treads, in the soffits of the foyer skylights and (renewed) lino floor, and in the timber supports of the hall gallery balustrade. Additions, some by Pike himself from 1973, have respected this integrity.

HULL COLLEGE

Queen's Gardens, Hull
1952–62; Frederick Gibberd

While it struggled to realise the rebuilding of the bombed city centre, in 1952 Hull City Council commissioned Gibberd to landscape the former Queen's Dock, infilled in 1937. At its head he created the college of technology, a nine-storey block of simple curtain walling interrupted by two set-back stair towers and topped by a zigzag roof, a feature seen in his public housing in the late 1950s. David Neave writes that it has 'an elegant simplicity'. The ground floor was originally glazed behind claw-like pilotis that formed a cloister, now infilled, with behind it an open exhibition area. Gibberd also made a feature of views from the roof. At the centre of the third floor is a decorative panel of concrete coloured with synthetic resin by William Mitchell, who was then working with Gibberd at Harlow Water Gardens and Liverpool Metropolitan Cathedral.

To the rear the single-storey technical workshops were the first element to be completed, in 1955, their north-facing roof lights set in sharp-tooth shell roofs. Gibberd added the Wilberforce Building (the College of Commerce) to the north in 1968 and the School of Art to the south in 1974, both part of the original plan. Unfortunately, trees now block his intended view from the sunken Queen's Gardens, which saw the college rising behind the Wilberforce Memorial (1834, moved here in 1935) above the former dock walls carved with reliefs by another sculptor who specialised in reliefs, Robert Adams. Further reliefs to the north are by Kenneth Carter from the college.

Hull

BOUSFIELD SCHOOL

South Bolton Gardens, Kensington, London
1954–56; Chamberlin, Powell & Bon
Listed grade II

Despite having the world's largest architect's department, the London County Council could not design all the schools it needed. Smaller commissions were passed outside, and this site near Powell's home came to CPB in 1952. In December the practice produced plans accommodating 240 infants and 320 juniors on the site of six war-damaged villas, one the former home of Beatrix Potter.

The school was planned in brick and concrete but as built had an external steel frame. The striking feature is an infilling of Pilkington glass panels demonstrating the principles of colour mixing, with yellow verticals, blue horizontals and green panels where the two meet. Aluminium windows were a spin-off from the aircraft industry. The school is arranged around two courtyards, with a single-storey range for infants to the south and a two-storey block for juniors to the north, with between them a pair of assembly halls, the kitchen and dining areas. An external amphitheatre was formed from a wartime water tank. The retention of mature trees led the architects to describe the school as 'a pavilion in a garden'.

Facing Boltons Place is a moat designed, Powell quipped, to keep out school inspectors. Elsewhere a brick wall matches the surrounding Victorian villas, pierced to allow views into the amphitheatre. Sprayed concrete was used for a circular water tank like a lollipop or Belisha beacon in the playground. For anyone who finds the Barbican hard and impersonal, the humanity of this little building is a reminder of the practice's warm heart.

SOUTHAMPTON UNIVERSITY

Highfield Campus, Southampton
1955–69; Basil Spence & Partners

Southampton is a Cinderella among university campuses, lacking the greenery of Nottingham or Exeter, and the brutalism of Sussex. Instead, a series of gentle, minimal buildings are woven around wartime huts and earlier workshops, or stand against a steep, more open landscape. The mix of natural materials and curtain walling is reminiscent of Le Corbusier's Pavillon Suisse, but the layout also acknowledges Mies van der Rohe's buildings for the Illinois Institute of Technology – visited by Spence's right-hand man, Jack Bonnington. Unlike these icons, the Southampton campus remains unrecognised and largely set for demolition.

Spence's first commission in June 1955 was to design the engineering building and a women's hall of residence. What followed was typical of universities in the 1950s, for the University Grants Committee then asked for a master plan, and Spence secured the commission with his charm and skilful perspectives. University Road bisects the campus. On the east side, Spence added a nine-storey tower and two slabs for engineering, in 1958–60, and a chemistry building (1960–63), creating courtyards with the older blocks. On the west side were more individual buildings. Spence commissioned F.E. McWilliams's sculpture *Puy de Dôme* as a centrepiece. Cut into the hillside, Geology/Botany and Physics (1964–66) are deceptively simple, while the Senior Common Room (1958–60) and Students' Union (1964–66) openly exhibit Bonnington's love of Mies, with heavy, exposed steel frames floating over larger brick masses concealed in the slope.

7 Lanchester Building

SWANSEA UNIVERSITY

Singleton Park, Sketty, Swansea
1957–63; Sir Percy Thomas & Son
Listed grade II

Swansea Technical College was admitted as a constituent part of the University of Wales in 1919 and the next year secured a site on the west side of the city at Singleton Abbey. By 1939 there were 65 staff and 485 students. The development of the campus truly began only in 1947 under its principal John Fulton, with a series of buildings still classical in form though modern in their details. It is as a group that they are remarkable, at a time when only Birmingham, Nottingham and Exeter really existed as campuses. The teaching buildings were joined by residential blocks to the rear.

Thomas's first and most important buildings make a formal core to the campus. First was the Natural Science Building, with alternating reliefs of an insect, boar, globe and such Welsh insignia as a daffodil. Fulton gave his name posthumously (in 1986) to the large, 'H'-shaped central administrative, dining and entertainment building erected in 1958–62 to the designs of Thomas's son, Norman. Misha Black decorated the main hall, which retains its original doors, panelling and light fittings. The mural at the west end, *The Rape of Europa* by Ceri Richards (1903–71, born and trained locally), was added in 1970 yet fits its setting well (shown on page 124). Again, it was a modern interpretation of a classical tradition – though Richards's wife Frances said that his source for the composition was a poem by Dylan Thomas, 'The Force that through the Green Fuse Drives the Flower'.

SCARBOROUGH TECHNICAL COLLEGE

Lady Edith's Drive, Scarborough, North Yorkshire
1958–61, extended 1967–68; Gollins, Melvin, Ward & Partners

No firm adopted American curtain walling with such aplomb and finesse as that of Gollins, Melvin, Ward & Partners. Gollins and Melvin had worked together for small commercial firms in the late 1930s but success came when they were joined by Edmund Ward after the Second World War. They designed the first London offices and showrooms in the genre, on New Cavendish Street – the new post-war centre of the rag trade – before going on to create some of its most prominent tower blocks. However, they had already designed many buildings for schools and higher education colleges, and in 1953 won a prestigious competition for additions to Sheffield University, mostly realised in the 1960s.

Technical colleges were always (and remain) the Cinderellas of higher education, dependent on local authorities for funding and often designed by the county surveyors. Not in the North Riding of Yorkshire, however, where the wily chief education officer, Frank Barraclough, employed leading specialist architects in the genre such as Denis Clarke Hall, Richard Sheppard and Birkin Haward, as well as GMW. Scarborough followed an earlier college in Middlesbrough but is now a lone survivor, though it is also set for demolition. If the style follows that of Mies van der Rohe in Chicago and Gordon Bunshaft in New York, the compact massing of tall classroom blocks with long, lower ranges of workshops more closely reflects the English picturesque. The clean lines unite these varied uses. A low block by the site entrance, used for teaching hairdressing, was added in 1967–68.

RAISED FACULTY BUILDINGS

Sidgwick Avenue, Cambridge
1958–64; Casson, Conder & Partners
Listed grade II

Today we can admire the precise, almost brutalist concrete, down to the crisp zigzags of the escape stairs and coal-black aggregate. But when, in 1952, Hugh Casson and Neville Conder won a limited competition to house the university's arts faculties it was because their modern scheme had one advantage over a classical design by Robert Atkinson & Partners: as it was asymmetrical it could be built in sections and not show if something never happened. The centrepiece is a cloistral building housing the English and language departments, with their respective libraries; smaller departments, called 'jokers', were edged out as these larger subjects grew and it is now all languages. The higher building to the west, in brick rather than Portland stone, is largely for economists. The double-height Marshall Library has a gallery supported on slim steel piers and some original sketches on display. Conder, the practice's chief designer, raised the complex on steps to deter bicycles.

At the entrance to the site are the more public halls, including the Lady Mitchell Hall, completed in 1964 (again in brick) only after much controversy and many revisions. The high mansards and monopitch roofs are typical of Conder's mature work. He also planned a mix of large and small buildings to the north, thwarted when householders refused to sell. Instead a piecemeal programme evolved over 40 years. Casson and Conder supported the building of James Stirling's History Faculty as a contrast to their own work, but subsequent large buildings are less well integrated.

ST CATHERINE'S COLLEGE

Manor Road, Oxford
1960–66; Arne Jacobsen
Listed grade I

Jacobsen is the master of mid-century modernism, his involvement at St Catherine's extending from its cutlery to the landscaping. Its charismatic warden, Alan Bullock, admired American architecture, but felt it was out of reach; however, he saw similarities in Danish modernism, which was closer to hand. 'The care over detail is something that other Danes show, but Jacobsen more so,' he claimed.

Appointed in 1959, Jacobsen visited Bullock at New College, whose long, open-ended court and circular lawn informed those at St Catherine's. Equally important was Bullock's detailed schedule, which determined much of the layout and use of brick. Jacobsen selected Uxbridge flints for their yellowish colour.

Jacobsen produced two parallel ranges of residential accommodation enclosing the site on its long sides, with individual buildings housing communal facilities down the middle. The northern end was blocked by the Senior and Junior Common Rooms either side of the kitchen. Covered walkways set between brick piers provided partial stops in the long north–south vistas, and had parallels in Jacobsen's schools. A long canal separated the college from the entrance drive, at whose pivot was a circular bicycle shed, which with the lawn in the main quadrangle were the principal non-linear elements. The bell tower gave crucial height. The college was extended in 1983 by Jacobsen's assistant, Knud Holscher, by Stephen Hodder in 1994–95 and 2002–05 (who also made alterations to Jacobsen's student accommodation) and Purcell in 2017–19.

TRADES UNION CONGRESS
TUC
TUC

PUBLIC BUILDINGS AND MEMORIALS

MEMORIAL GARDENS

Church Hill, Walsall, West Midlands
1951–52, 1954–60; Geoffrey Jellicoe
Landscape registered grade II

Medieval Walsall, a once-proud hilltop citadel, was demolished as a slum in the 1930s, leaving only the church of St Matthew. In its place, the town commissioned Jellicoe to create a memorial garden commemorating the dead of both world wars, begun in May 1951 when Princess Margaret laid a foundation stone. He created a walled garden, richly planted and largely turned in on itself as a tranquil space for contemplation, entered through small gateways with classical broken pediments. Windows in the walls giving views across the Black Country have similar pediments, and little balconies that in a modern guise became a regular feature of Jellicoe's work. An open terrace is now a private garden for the gardener's cottage, first occupied by the local police commissioner and in separate ownership since its restoration in 1998.

At the other end of the garden the copper roofs of the memorial chapel appear as a gazebo against the walls. It was actually the last part of the scheme to be completed, a date of around 1960 reflected in its concrete mullions and pilotis. The steps and cobbles that line the route up the steep hill are also part of this phase, anticipating Jellicoe's interpretation of the Pilgrim's Progress in the Kennedy Memorial at Runnymede. But in between, Jellicoe realised his last works as a housing specialist before concentrating on landscape, designing a delightfully decorative terrace of old people's flats in 1954 faced in brick and render, and the Brotherhood (parish) Hall for St Matthew's.

St. Matthews
Close
St. Matthews
Close

CONGRESS HOUSE

Great Russell Street, London
1954–58; David du Roi Aberdeen
Listed grade II*

This office block and conference hall is slightly out of time, for the design won a competition in 1948, although construction did not begin until building licensing ended. It defines the mid-century style at its most monumental, conceived as a war memorial to trades unionists from the armed forces and civilians alike. The Trades Union Congress built it as their headquarters and an education centre.

The central bombsite was chosen because it could be reached from across Britain. It was narrow and deep, however, and next door reared the blank party wall of Edwin Lutyens's overweening YWCA. Aberdeen first conceived a tower block in the manner of Rio de Janeiro's Ministry of Education building, but realised that the brick wall would still dominate. Instead he pulled the disparate elements into a compact scheme around three sides of a courtyard over a top-lit, basement conference hall, demonstrating how a building of similar height but in a thoroughly modern style could be an exemplary neighbour. It demonstrated the natural light and good working conditions for which the TUC campaigned, as well as magnificent British craftsmanship and materials. The fourth side was Lutyens's wall, which became a setting (now modified) for a war memorial, designed by Jacob Epstein as a working man's *pietà* when another competition produced no winners. A commended sculptor, Bernard Meadows (an assistant of Henry Moore), did produce *The Spirit of Brotherhood*, the bronze over the main entrance depicting the strong helping the weak.

CENTRAL PARADE

Hoe Street, Walthamstow, London
1955–58; F.G. Southgate, borough surveyor
Listed grade II

If one building exemplifies mid-century modern in Britain, this is it. The symbol of Walthamstow's resurgence after a V-1 rocket hit the crossroads in the heart of the town, there is the inevitable post-war clock tower. There is also a viewing platform, as well as a bank, offices, shops, 31 flats and a community hall all packed into an 'L'-shaped block. The council's plans for such an exceptional range of facilities date to the early 1950s, encouraged by an enthusiastic alderman, Ross Wyld. The early date may also explain the decoration. The tower and viewing platform buzz with geometric tiles supplied by Carter's of Poole. Special tiles form heraldic plaques commemorating Walthamstow's ancient families – the Monnox, Tonis and Maynards, whose symbols reappear in mosaic as the borough coat of arms with its motto by William Morris (raised locally) that tops the tower. They contrast with red brickwork, artificial stone, green slate panels and concrete, including wavy shell canopies – now painted yellow, as if more colour was needed, with steel and concrete balconies to the flats. The corner bank later became a library and is now a café. The hall (originally named after Wyld) retains its woodblock floors, stage and signage.

Unusually for a borough surveyor, F.G. Southgate was a qualified architect, specialising in housing, though the design was probably made by his young assistants S.W. Nash, D.E. Hill and G.W. Kew. Central Parade is fun, but also fulfils its purpose of giving Walthamstow an identity.

CENTRAL
PARADE
CHURCH HILL

HARINGEY CIVIC CENTRE

High Street, Wood Green, London
1955–58; John Sayers of Sir John Brown, A. E. Henson & Partners
Listed grade II

Wood Green's was the first town hall built from scratch after the Second World War. The architects had won a competition in 1939 for a traditional design replacing an earlier hall at Woodside Park, but after 1945 the borough council found a new site – intending to add public halls and a library, which were never realised. Only the first of three intended phases was built, resulting in large amounts of handsome ceremonial space but few offices.

The new design by Sayers shows the work of a younger generation. There is a strong Danish influence, with echoes of Arne Jacobsen and Erik Møller's Aarhus City Hall (1938–41) and Jacobsen's Søllerød City Hall of 1939–42 (with Flemming Lassen) in the use of simple forms and refined materials. The large entrance hall is lined in Florentine travertine marble, used also for the treads of the helical staircase, behind which the timber panels are lined in gold; the effect shows it is clearly cladding, as Scandinavian designers were keen to highlight. The council chamber is lined with *Verte de Fre* marble, while the cocktail cabinet in the mayoral suite is lined in Ashburton marble. Travertine was used for the registry office; elsewhere there is English straight-grained elm panelling, but best of all, perhaps, is the council chamber's concertina ceiling, an arc of stepped coved lighting. The horseshoe seating was removed in 1965, when Wood Green was merged with Tottenham and Hornsey to become the larger London Borough of Haringey, but the bench seating in the public gallery survives.

CIVIC CENTRE

Barras Bridge, Newcastle upon Tyne
1956–68; George W. Kenyon, city architect
Listed grade II*

A new city hall was designed in 1939 but abandoned in the war. New plans were prepared in 1950 but renewing the city's housing stock took priority, so the council allowed Kenyon to prepare a design that could be realised slowly, construction beginning in 1956. It is thus a building out of time, its Scandinavian qualities recognised when it was opened by no less a dignitary than Olav V, King of Norway, but not appreciated elsewhere. Artworks and rich materials contribute hugely to the success of the architecture.

The Civic Centre is part office building, part function suite. First came the Rates Hall range at the rear, opened in 1960, the hall with murals by Victor Pasmore, then teaching in Newcastle. Next followed a 12-storey central office range and finally the imposing council chamber and public hall fronting Barras Bridge, where the sculptural enrichment was most lavish. Local artists were used for the first phases, but more famous names were later introduced. The centre is approached via the Ceremonial Way, with nine flambeaux by Charles Sansbury, who designed metal screens to the internal courtyard and, inside, the lift doors. The banqueting hall features a John Piper tapestry. The entrance is dominated by *River God Tyne* by David Wynne, with next to it a carillon tower, the most Scandinavian feature culminating in copper fins sporting seahorses and crowns from the city's coat of arms. The Civic Centre remains an exceptional civic ensemble of art and architecture, but was radically altered in 2018–20.

LILLINGTON LIBRARY

Valley Road, Lillington, Leamington Spa, Warwickshire
1959–60; Henry Fedeski
Listed grade II

A new housing estate appeared in the 1950s at Lillington, a village just outside Leamington Spa. Its centre was an attractive shopping precinct, with nearby a Catholic church and library. The architect of both was Henry Fedeski (1907–93) of Rayner & Fedeski, born and raised in Warwickshire despite his foreign-sounding name, and who built a curiously classical house for himself nearby. The church of 1962–63 has a spectacular interior, centrally planned and glazed with *dalle de verre* by Dom Charles Norris of Buckfast Abbey.

The earlier library alongside is charmingly childlike and truly idiosyncratic. Its distinctive feature is the chequerboard gable of two first-floor flats, one intended for the librarian; designed to give height and prominence to the little building, they project over angled concrete piers. The materials are many and varied, the pale brick and concrete enlivened with Hornton stone, slate and aggregate panels in grey and lemon yellow, with full-height glazing to the library itself and a copper roof. Small extensions have not detracted from the audacity of the main facade. The interior by contrast is plain, designed for easy supervision by a lone librarian.

The building was designed as early as 1953, which may explain the Festival style, but government restrictions on capital public works delayed its building – so many libraries around the country were delayed in this way that the Library Association attacked the lack of investment compared with schools and housing. In the interim the council operated a service from a redundant police station in the village.

Library

BT TOWER / POST OFFICE TOWER

Cleveland Mews, London
1961–65; Ministry of Public Buildings and Works
Listed grade II

The 1950s saw the rapid growth in sales of telephones and televisions, more than could be connected by cabling. Radio telephones using low frequencies had long been in operation but the development of high frequencies was in its infancy. Experiments had focused on the Museum Telephone Exchange, which served Broadcasting House and a television transmitter, when in 1952 it was chosen as the centre of a national network of aerials. The new tower had to be high enough to be seen by the next transmitters, at Hampstead and Alexandra Palace, and – as tall buildings began to appear in London – its proposed height was raised twice before 580ft (177m) (plus a 39ft/12m mast) was settled on. Stability was crucial to the accuracy of the transmitters, mounted on circular galleries for maximum flexibility and to reduce wind resistance, so the tower was braced to the adjoining office block.

Only a small public observation platform was first planned, but this was reconsidered in 1960 following the success of the restaurant on top of the television tower in Stuttgart (1956) and of the revolving Florianturm in Dortmund (1959). The restaurant and observation towers, with kitchens on top, went massively over budget but added further stability.

The Post Office Tower symbolised the space race, the panoramic globe on top resembling an artificial satellite, while the lifts were Britain's fastest. It attracted 4.6 million visitors before a bomb explosion in 1971 forced the observation decks to close; the restaurant closed in 1980, though its revolving floor survives.

HORNSEY LIBRARY

Haringey Park, Crouch End, London
1963–65; Frank Ley and G.F.S. Jarvis
Listed grade II

Public libraries underwent enormous changes in the 1950s. The introduction of plastic covers from America enabled decorative book jackets to be preserved, while the books themselves (especially those for children) became more colourful. New buildings were bigger and lighter, mainly due to innovations from Denmark, a place of pilgrimage for librarians. Frederiksberg Library, opened in 1935, had featured a double-height lending hall where a gallery for the less popular books had freed up the main floor for exhibitions, events and informal seating.

In London this plan first appeared in 1960 at Holborn Library, along with special reference rooms and a lecture hall. Holborn retains some mid-century features, including Formica panels and a mosaic, but otherwise Hornsey Library is better preserved. Where Holborn stacked its facilities one above the other, behind the town hall at Hornsey there was space to place the double-height lending library on one side of a wide entrance and the reference library and lecture hall on the other, set above a large (and recently extended) children's library.

The library was the last building erected by (Conservative) Hornsey Borough Council, spending its reserves before in 1965 it merged with (Labour) Wood Green and Tottenham to form Haringey. It commemorates the borough in an etched window by Frederick Mitchell and a fountain by T.B. Huxley-Jones. Best, however, are the building's two cranked, cantilevered staircases and the colourful old bookcases, especially those under the butterfly roof in the reference library.

CROSBY LIBRA
& CIVIC HAL

CROSBY LIBRARY

Crosby Road North, Waterloo, Merseyside
1964–68; G. Ronald Mason, borough architect

Crosby's was to be a new type of library: bold, lively and forward-looking. Yet architecturally it belongs as much to the 1950s as the 1960s, with its blond brick, large windows and a projecting staircase drum topped by a Scandinavian-style beacon. It shows how public buildings were a bastion of mid-century modern into the 1960s, partly because of the long process of approving plans and securing loans, partly because the style lent itself to civic dignity and partly because it remained popular, especially where no complicated engineering was required. But being unfashionable ensured that these buildings were never published in the architectural magazines and still receive little save local recognition.

The main adult library occupies the long 'nave' of the building, a double-height main space with a gallery for reference collections and less frequently borrowed books, as made popular by Holborn. Less altered than Holborn, the hanging pendant lights are original, featured in the architect's sketches from 1968 held in the library archives. To one side, the low children's library had its own entrance. To the rear, a civic hall was added in 1974–75, designed for amateur dramatics, with meeting rooms for local societies. They have their own entrance from the drum. Such a variety of provision contrasted with the sedate Carnegie Library of 1904–06 which it superseded, but which was converted into a community centre in 2015.

FULLWELL CROSS LIBRARY

High Street, Barkingside, Greater London
1965–67; Frederick Gibberd
Listed grade II

Already well established at Harlow, 20 miles (32km) away, Frederick Gibberd was a natural choice when Essex County Council rejected a design by Ilford Borough Council's in-house engineer for a new branch library. Fullwell Cross, the gateway to Essex, had developed as a commuter suburb with the building of Eastern Avenue, but its only library was a converted shop. Gibberd agreed to produce plans and elevations in September 1958, but changes to the brief for an adjoining swimming pool, which he also designed, and local government reorganisation that saw Ilford become part of the London Borough of Redbridge in 1965 caused long delays.

The library's plan, with its double-height, round central hall, resembles in miniature Gibberd's Liverpool Metropolitan Cathedral, but was designed some months earlier in 1959. The low entrance leads into a high, circular lending library, where the place of the altar is taken by the panopticon issue desk of the all-seeing librarian. The bookshelves radiate from this centre with beyond them, at the end of the axis, a lower reference room. The building marks a shift in Gibberd's style towards an emphasis on bold shapes and simple detailing, realised in pale concrete panels. The ground floor with its artfully alternating pattern of punched windows shows this well. Higher up, the transition is not completed, for the dome over the main lending library is formed of a series of ribbed shell cones clad in copper, leaving at their ends round-headed windows to the high clerestory that impart a quaintly Middle Eastern touch.

Fullwell Cross Library

THE CLOCK HOUSE
Traditional Free House

SHOPS, OFFICES AND INDUSTRY

BANKSIDE POWER STATION

Southwark, London
1947–60; Sir Giles Gilbert Scott

Bankside is a monumental piece of massing and fine brickwork that is Scott's finest non-religious building. It was built on the site of a pioneering power station (1883) damaged during the Second World War.

Bankside's single 300ft (91m) chimney is a striking counterpoise to the dome of St Paul's opposite, indebted to Dutch brick modernism but simplified during the design process. Anxiety about the destructive effects of smoke on the historic cathedral fabric led engineers to devise a special plant to produce a 'smokeless shimmer of vapour'; this is thought to have drifted lower and caused more damage. The government demanded that the power station be oil-fired, a factor in Bankside's early redundancy in 1980, and on the electricity industry's privatisation it was granted to Nuclear Electric as an asset. When listing for the building was refused a second time in 1992, demolition seemed inevitable. In desperation, the Twentieth Century Society encouraged architects and engineers to produce ideas for the building's reuse, which achieved good publicity.

The Tate Gallery saw the possibilities and intervened. It held an international architectural competition to convert the power station into a gallery for its modern collection, won by the Swiss architects Herzog & de Meuron. The elevation was further simplified, cutting out its projecting centrepiece, while only the main internal space recalls the cathedral-like quality of the original – but it is a striking success, and the one survivor out of dozens of 1950s power stations.

THE WORLD
THANK YOU KEY
TATE MODERN

HOUSE OF FRASER
HOUSE OF FRASER

HAMMONDS

Ferensway, Hull
1950–52; T.P. Bennett & Son

Hull had the dubious privilege of having Britain's most bomb-damaged city centre, though part had been cleared already to build a new street, Ferensway. Patrick Abercrombie produced an ambitious plan, with a new railway station and shopping area north of Queen's Gardens. The city corporation struggled to implement the proposals; the railway refused to move and the Chamber of Trade commissioned an alternative plan from a rival planner, W.R. Davidge.

Stalemate still prevailed when the first government allocation of steel arrived in 1948. In stepped Hammonds department store, ready to build after fighting the corporation to keep its pre-war site opposite Paragon Station. H.W. Hammond had opened a drapery store in 1821, sold in 1889 to James Powell and his three sons, who built a department store on the present site in 1916. This was destroyed in May 1941 but the shop continued to trade in temporary premises.

T.P. Bennett & Son designed the replacement store, opened in May 1952. The Powells demanded a semi-traditional style so shoppers could recognise elements of the old store with its giant order of columns. This led to triple-height columns on the corner facade, with Art Deco wavelets in the glazing until it was changed in c. 2010. Additions followed in 1957, including a restaurant, and in 1960. Taken over by the House of Fraser in 1972, Hammonds had assumed the chain's generic name by the time of its closure in August 2019. In 2020 it was remodelled as an artisan food hall with new glazing and signage.

BROADGATE HOUSE

Broadgate, Coventry
1948–53; Coventry City Architect's Department, under Donald Gibson
Listed grade II

This was the first element to be realised of Gibson's plan for central Coventry, which was pioneering for its pedestrian shopping precinct. The main thoroughfare, angled on the cathedral, has been altered despite partial listing. On the square, an 'L'-shaped block of offices over shops – Broadgate House – survives better.

Princess Elizabeth laid the foundation stone for the first range in May 1948. This follows the rational style adopted by Gibson in sketches from 1942, indebted to Lewis Mumford's *The Culture of Cities* but an unusual stripped classicism for post-war Britain that is curiously reminiscent of totalitarian Italy. By contrast, the south side affirms the British romanticism of mid-century modernism, fulfilling a stated aim of creating a building completely of 1953. It commemorates Lady Godiva, said to have ridden through Coventry naked behind her long hair to fulfil a wager after her husband Leofric imposed repressive tolls on the city. She entreated the townsfolk not to look, but was spied on by Peeping Tom.

A bell was salvaged when the old market was bombed in 1940; hence the significance of the clock tower. On the hour Lady Godiva appears on a white horse, overlooked by leering Peeping Tom in his old vest. Their artist, Gibson's friend Trevor Tennant, carved more figures facing Hertford Street, which cut through the building until 1968. A mosaic in the office entrance designed by Hugh Hosking and realised by René Antonietti commemorates the Protestant Coventry Martyrs – again the city reaffirming its history by pictorial means.

rtford Street
SHOPPING
Lady Godiva News
Devlins
& Wine
Tobacconists Newsagents
CORAL
THE ASYLUM
OPEN

HERMÈS
HERMÈS
Loro Piana

TIME AND LIFE BUILDING

153–7 New Bond Street, London
1951–53; Michael Rosenauer
Listed grade II*

On a bombsite in the heart of London's bustling West End, two buildings were erected ahead of the relaxation of building licensing because they were paid for with American dollars. One was the Westbury Hotel, kept deliberately understated. The other was the exuberant headquarters of Time Life International. Rosenauer was an Austrian émigré who had spent the Second World War in New York, where he evolved his earlier expertise in compact flats to plan offices and hotels. Time and Life is virtually free-standing – a roof terrace between it and its neighbour ensures there was no need for a dank light well.

More importantly, Time and Life has a remarkable assemblage of British art. Henry Moore collaborated with Rosenauer on an external screen of four colossal abstract figures, and for the roof terrace created a *Draped Reclining Figure*. Over the entrance is a bronze sculpture, *The Symbol of Community*, by Maurice Lambert, and inside an iron relief by Geoffrey Clarke has been moved to the foyer. The interiors were commissioned from Hugh Casson, who reassembled the core of his Festival team, to show here that they could work with rich materials and produce serious modern designs. He and Misha Black designed a double-height reception space, now subdivided. Leonard Manasseh and H.T. Cadbury-Brown created the executive suites, and R.Y. Goodden a balustrade finished in black leather, tooled and patterned with brass studs, which is now all that survives. Murals by Oliver Cox in the cafeteria offered the greatest note of gaiety.

FORMER LEWIS'S DEPARTMENT STORE

Ranelagh Street, Liverpool
1951–53, 1954–57; Gerald de Courcy Fraser,
succeeded by Fraser, Sons & Geary
Listed grade II

Not to be confused with the John Lewis chain, few department stores were as grand as Lewis's of Liverpool, founded in 1856 by David Lewis and which became the flagship of a nationwide chain that in the 1950s included London's Selfridges. It was rebuilt in classical style by de Courcy Fraser in 1910–23, and again after this was destroyed in the Second World War. The entrance was completed in 1956 with Jacob Epstein's male nude, *Liverpool Resurgent*, known for obvious reasons as 'Dickie Lewis', with relief panels symbolising 'the new Liverpool' based on sketches of his own children and grandchildren.

The interior featured marble hallways and Art Deco staircases, with fluted columns derived from those at Selfridges. Best was the fifth floor, housing a hair salon and restaurants, abandoned in 1987 but lingering in decrepit splendour until the store closed in 2010. The cafeteria seating 300 people was tiled by Carter's of Poole in 1953, for whom Alfred Burgess Read specialised in depictions of food and crockery; he may have designed the 60ft (18.3m) mural set behind the servery. Other walls have a knife and fork or wave motifs, while hanging lights and metal screens reinforce the Festival idiom. In 2020 it was the breakfast room to a hotel, though this may change in plans to reopen the ground floor. There were also originally two waitress-service dining rooms alongside. The sculptor Mitzi Cunliffe recovered her metal screen from the Red Rose Restaurant, but wooden panelling incised with local scenes by Susan Einzig survives from the Mersey Room.

BEALES
BEALES
DEPARTMENT STORES
BEALES

BEALES

Old Christchurch Road, Bournemouth
1952–56; Jackson & Greenen

John Elmes Beale of Weymouth opened his 'Fancy Fair and Oriental House' in 1881, just as the town was growing as a resort. The enterprise thrived, expanding on to a three-sided block in the heart of the town that was mostly raised and refronted in a gaunt Art Deco style in 1931. It burned down in May 1943 when the Luftwaffe hit a nearby gas pipe. Reconstruction commenced in 1952, well recorded by the builders Drewitts.

The new building was similarly gaunt and ship-like. It forms a simple, bold curve to the corner of Old Christchurch Road, its narrow bands of horizontal glazing on the upper floors contrasted with brickwork and bookended by staircase towers to either side clad in smart grey and yellow tiles, some of them in stripes. The entrance, with its display cabinets to either side, was remodelled more simply after another fire, in 1966.

Gordon Jackson studied architecture in his native Glasgow before moving to Bournemouth, where in 1922 he formed a partnership with Wallace A. Greenen. The practice was continued from 1953 by his son Alec Walter Jackson.

The Bournemouth store became the flagship of a national chain that expanded in the 1960s. It took on more shops in the 2000s and, more surprisingly, in 2011 – but with them came a large debt that proved unsustainable as shoppers drifted away from traditional high street stores. The Bournemouth store finally closed in March 2020 and, although it is in a Conservation Area, its future is uncertain.

GROSVENOR HOUSE

Bennett's Hill and New Street, Birmingham
1953–54; Cotton, Ballard and Blow
Listed grade II

Jack Cotton was a prominent Birmingham estate agent and property developer who advanced from building housing estates to speculating in office schemes. In the post-war years he was behind much of the rebuilding of Birmingham city centre from a suite at London's Dorchester Hotel, his office laid out across the spare bed, before overreaching himself with ambitious schemes in London and New York. Unusually, he also ran his own architectural practice, with Blow the one qualified partner. Most of its buildings were unexceptional, save at Southsea (see page 204), and in 1960 Cotton brought in Walter Gropius to add gravitas to a controversial scheme for rebuilding the Monico Café at London's Piccadilly Circus. Grosvenor House is the exception, and one of very few speculative offices to be listed.

The *Architects' Journal* suggested in 1954 that the jaunty elevations might have come from Paris, though in practice the zigzag bays were a means of maximising the site, each one cantilevered over the pavement. Projecting sills contrast with the ripple of the windows, topped by a projecting cornice, meeting in a double prow at the corner with a little round bay. This is a rare and delightful example of the 'contemporary' style at its most energetic, which survives externally little altered. It seems still more surprising in Birmingham, a city more associated with the 1960s. Built when office buildings were still strictly controlled by licences, with shops on the ground floor, it was first occupied by Shell-Mex BP – one of the growth firms of the 1950s.

ASK ITALIAN
TO LET

ODHAMS PRESS HALL

St Albans Road, Watford, Hertfordshire
1954–57; Yates, Cook and Darbyshire

Odhams were leading printers in the mid-century years, producing magazines that promoted the style. William Odhams set up business in about 1847 as a London printer, selling the firm in 1892 to his two sons, who appointed Julius Elias as managing director. The firm assumed the name Odhams Press in 1920 when they took over the *John Bull* magazine in return for bad debts. Expansion followed, acquiring a majority share in the *Daily Herald*, and magazines including *Ideal Home* and *Horse & Hound*. In 1935 it built a dedicated high-speed photogravure and colour works on wasteland at Watford, chosen for its excellent road and rail links. The result of its expansion was *Woman*, the first colour weekly magazine, and a second factory followed in 1939. Odhams extended the premises in 1954 with the multi-storey No.4 Building, the striking clock tower to the press hall housing a substantial water tank.

Odhams's fortunes turned when Cecil Harmsworth King, chairman of the *Daily Mirror* group, made a successful takeover bid, and in 1963 the combined holdings amalgamated with those of the George Newnes group and others to form the International Publishing Corporation (IPC). The name Odhams continued until January 1969, publishing boys' comics, whence the newly expanded works turned to printing the *Sunday Mirror*. The complex was closed by Robert Maxwell in 1983 following the arrival of cheaper lithographic printing. The frontage building and clock tower is all that survives; the rest was demolished for an ASDA supermarket.

SUGAR SILO

Regent Road, Liverpool
1955–57; Tate & Lyle Engineer's Department
Listed grade II*

Concrete's great strength meant that it was quickly adopted for storing unstable loads such as grain, and the iconic silos erected around Buffalo, New York, were lovingly published by Walter Gropius and Le Corbusier, and actually visited by Erich Mendelsohn.

In the 1920s, Imperial Chemicals realised that a parabolic arched construction followed the natural shape of a mound of loose material – in their case, fertiliser – and was therefore even stronger. They took their cue from Eugene Freyssinet's airship hangars at Orly (1916–24, demolished). David Bailey of Tate & Lyle adopted the same principle to store sugar for its Liverpool refinery nearby. Erected in 12 sections using a wooden scaffold into which concrete was poured over a steel frame, at 528ft (161m) long and 87ft (26.5m) high it was the largest parabolic silo in England – larger than the similar silos built for storing salt by Pier Luigi Nervi at Tortona, Italy, in 1950–51. Raw sugar was loaded via a system of conveyor belts from the dockside, rising even higher than the silo, then reclaimed by gravity through a line of hoppers into another conveyor set below a pre-stressed floor – the structure is deep as well as tall. It has more recently been used for storing grain.

Tate & Lyle closed their Love Lane refinery in 1981, and today the silo is owned by the Mersey Docks and Peel Ports. There have been proposals to use it for concerts, and a one-off event was held there in 2003.

PRIMARK
PRIMARK
NO ENTRY
TAKE CARE
STAY SAFE

STEVENAGE TOWN CENTRE

Stevenage, Hertfordshire

1955–59; Leonard Vincent, Stevenage Development Corporation

Clock tower listed grade II

Stevenage was Britain's first new town, designated in November 1946 to relieve London's overcrowding. It was also Britain's first pedestrianised town centre. The American architect-planner Clarence Stein produced proposals in 1950 which were adapted by the British planner Gordon Stephenson and the corporation architect Clifford Holliday. But then came opposition from the leading chain stores, led by Woolworths, and it was only thanks to a local campaign in 1954 that a pedestrian scheme won out. The sheltering canopies owe something to an earlier design by Peter Shepheard, but Vincent determined the simple grid of the facades, which he conceived as a backdrop to the shops' signage, much more elaborate then than today. Building extended from Southgate as far north as Park Place by 1959, resuming in 1962–64 (in heavier concrete) with a restaurant on a bridge over the main Queensway. Gyula Bajó, a Hungarian-born artist, designed the tile mural on the south side of the main square for the Letchworth, Hitchin and District Co-operative Society, the first store to open in the new town centre in June 1958.

The Queen unveiled the clock tower and fountains in April 1959. The clock is made of Perspex, below which is a tile map by Carter & Co. with decorative tiles by Peggy Angus and a bust of Lewis Silkin, the minister responsible for the new towns. The same artist, Franta Belsky from Czechoslovakia, also designed the nearby sculpture *Joy Ride*, a mother and child he described as 'a happy new town riding on the back of the old'.

MARKET SQUARE

Harlow, Essex
1955–60; Frederick Gibberd and Partners

Of all London's early overspill new towns, Harlow was the most completely 'new'. Old Harlow became an isolated spur while new development spread westwards, with a commercial centre at the highest point. Here Gibberd created a network of pedestrian squares within a ring of service roads and car parks. The first, Market Square, reveals his fascination with the 19th-century Austrian Camillo Sitte, whose celebration of the Renaissance cities of northern Italy was a major influence on mid-century picturesque planning. Gibberd read it ahead of its first English edition in 1945. He himself wrote of traffic-free squares as a sequence of linked rooms, where the sky formed the ceiling.

Building began here in May 1955 because it was closest to new housing in Little Parndon and Hare Street, and the first shops opened that Christmas. A market with bright awnings, larger shops and the Painted Lady public house followed in May 1956. Particularly lively is a first-floor section modelled on The Rows at Chester, which included Gibberd's own office. He explained the need to provide such services as hairdressers' salons, 'but I really designed it just to give pleasure'. Following Sitte's exemplar of Verona's Piazza delle Erbe, he related public buildings to the shops and placed statues against a background or a vista rather than blocking a building's entrance. This is exemplified by *Meat Porters*, a homage to London's old Smithfield Market sited in 1960 alongside the colourful Adams House with its over-scaled clock – itself added as a focal point in 1957.

THE CLOCK HOUSE
Traditional Free House
THE CLOCK HOUSE
THE CLOCK HOUSE
Traditional Free Hous

JOHN LEWIS & PARTNERS
JOHN LEWIS & PARTNERS

JOHN LEWIS & PARTNERS

Oxford Street, London
1955–60; Reginald Uren of Slater & Uren
1961–63, *Winged Figure* by Barbara Hepworth listed grade II

John Spedan Lewis, son of the company's founder, had rebuilt a subsidiary store, Peter Jones, before turning to Oxford Street. There, Charles Reilly of Liverpool University had pushed his protégé William Crabtree over Lewis's preferred specialists, Slater & Moberly, later Slater & Uren. Lewis tolerated the self-important Crabtree until 1945, allowing him to produce streamlined glass schemes for Oxford Street, while Reilly saw off an approach from Erich Mendelsohn, the master of modernist shop design. But when Lewis rebuilt the rear block on Cavendish Square, he chose Arthur Moberly's conservative design of Portland stone and small windows rather than irritate the landowner, the Howard de Walden Estate.

Lewis had hesitated to replace his father's oriental Oxford Street frontage until an oil bomb exploded there in 1940. An in-house team erected a temporary store from materials salvaged on site to avoid licensing. Work began only in 1955 on a permanent emporium, less innovative than Peter Jones and with a large lightwell – though artificial lighting was then favoured for department stores, natural daylight is now John Lewis's greatest joy. Reginald Uren, the New Zealand architect of Hornsey Town Hall, produced a monumental design relieved by yellow tiles and grey slate to give a Scandinavian flavour. In 1960, the building complete, the partnership invited six artists to propose a sculpture for the corner of Holles Street. Instead, dissatisfied, it turned to Barbara Hepworth, whose aluminium *Winged Figure*, imparting the sensation of freedom, was installed in April 1963.

NATIONAL PROVINCIAL BANK

St Andrew's Cross, Plymouth
1956–59; Brian C. Sherren, Alan E. Souter and George F. Miles
Listed grade II

St Andrew's Cross marks the eastern end of Plymouth's city centre, the earliest and most coherent wholesale post-war reconstruction thanks to the dynamism of the city engineer James Paton Watson (1898–1979). Its uniform frontages of Portland stone, by a variety of outside architects mainly from London, are relieved by areas of colour, reliefs and the framing of the upper windows.

To terminate the main Royal Parade something more dynamic was needed, and the city gave the National Provincial Bank a free hand. Since the 1920s, it had produced the most interesting architecture of all the clearing banks, and Sherren, F. Norman James and their team continued a tradition set by Frederick Charles Palmer and Walter Holden. Post-war banks combined modernism with symbols of stability and tradition in their choice of materials and decoration, although here the cladding panels are remarkably varied and consciously expressed as a veneer. The granite columns of the square portico stand sharp against a background of turquoise mosaic, while the curved copper roof is crowned by a clock tower of blue glass. The detailed ornamentation celebrates the heritage of Plymouth and the bank itself, with gold emblems in the mosaic and in the glass side doors, while the bronze front doors are studded with roundels based on ancient coins. Such stripped yet richly decorated classicism, its sources in 1920s Scandinavia and Italy, was rarely realised and never so colourfully. St Petersburg's surprisingly similar Finland Station is slightly later.

KNIGHT & LEE
A BRANCH OF THE JOHN LEWIS PARTNERSHIP
No cycling or
skate boarding
past this point

KNIGHT & LEE

Palmerston Road, Southsea, Hampshire
1956–59; Cotton, Ballard and Blow

The 1950s were a golden age for department stores and Knight & Lee is among the finest, a fitting corner to Palmerston Road. The smaller shops on Southsea's premier high street were rebuilt by the city council itself to stimulate trade as early as 1950, to which maisonettes were added on top in brick and concrete patterns a year later. Handley's stolid department store followed in 1951–55, delayed by steel shortages.

Cotton, Ballard and Blow's rebuilding of Knight & Lee was altogether livelier. The main part dates from 1956–57, the extension down Clarendon Road from 1958–59. Of modest size, it has just the right balance of concrete frame, glass and brick, with diaper patterning to the stair tower and green slate to the ground floor. It also retained its original signage (as Knight & Lee rather than the John Lewis Partnership) until its closure in 2019.

The store had its origins in 1887 when brothers-in-law Jesse Knight and Edward Lee took on an existing millinery business and expanded it to specialise in boys' and menswear. John Lewis bought the business in 1933, among the first stores in its programme of expansion outside London, and it quickly prospered, until war damage in 1940 was followed by complete destruction in January 1941. The business took on temporary premises in Palmerston Arcade until the new store was completed. In 2021 Knight & Lee is set for major alterations to become a street food market, with a hotel and cinema on the upper floors.

PANNIER MARKET

Plymouth
1959; H.F. Walls and C.H.P. Pearn
Listed grade II

Plymouth's first market was built in 1804–07, its stalls later cleared away to create an informal 'pannier' market (traditionally based on baskets or panniers and popular in Devon). It was rebuilt in 1853 and altered again in 1891. It survived raids on the city in 1941, when such were the losses elsewhere that even Woolworths and Marks & Spencer took stalls. Recognising the importance of the market to Plymouth in the war, the rebuilding of the centre included a new market on a separate site and the old market finally closed on 5 September 1959 with a firework display.

The opening of the new market marked the completion of the rebuilt city centre. The interior remains impressive with six lofty shell vaults just 2½in (6.35cm) thick, created by the specialist Polish engineer Albin Chronowicz. The seven thick portal frames are connected by a ring beam that stops the roof from spreading, and northern lights cast an even natural light. A gallery café is reached by cantilevered stairs at either end. The spacing of the stalls was determined by tubular steel frames angled to an open pyramid and connected by steel rings (which survive) holding light fittings. The city architect Hector J.W. Stirling intended to produce the design, with a conference centre and exhibition hall, but pressure of work saw it passed to a local firm. Paul Pearn was the partner in charge and Ken Bingham the project architect, while their friend David Weeks embellished the entrances with reliefs.

AVENUE
1

Birds
This store is now closed.
Lister Gate
This store is now closed.

BIRDS BAKERY

4 The Poultry, Nottingham
1961; United Shopfitters of Bristol
Listed grade II

The diarist Celia Fiennes noted in 1697 how one side of Nottingham's Market Square was lined with a stone arcade, which was then repeated on all three sides. Although all the buildings have been replaced, most have repeated the feature in some form, so that there is some shelter for shoppers from the overhanging upper storeys supported on columns. But only one shop has two columns clad in blue and white mosaic. Behind it a curved glass shop front stretches from floor to ceiling, its double doors and display sections framed in chrome. The party wall is faced in red, grey and white mosaic. Above, the 'Birds' sign has the original looping script that growing up in the 1960s was the byword for fresh cream cakes on Friday teatimes. Birds' cakes were seriously good: the cream went all the way to the end in the cream horns, and leavened the tartness of blackcurrants in its succulent fruit tarts.

Frank, Thomas and Reginald Bird invested their ex-servicemen's gratuities to open a confectioner's shop in Derby in 1919, and had several branches there by 1939. No.4 The Poultry marked their descendants' first expansion into Nottingham, and more branches quickly followed in the surrounding small towns (reaching my native Beeston c. 1966). Their delicate glass display shelving, pendant lights and signage changed little until a heavy-handed refurbishment programme in 2017 followed a change of name from Birds the Confectioners to Birds Bakery, save at the central Nottingham branch, but this closed in 2020.

THREE SHIPS MURAL

Co-operative Store, Jameson Street, Hull
1961–63; Alan Boyson, on building by G.S. Hay, Co-operative Wholesale Society
Listed grade II

A new department store for the Kingston upon Hull Co-operative Society was a centrepiece of the city's rebuilt shopping area. But which way should it face? Construction began in 1956 facing south in accordance with Abercrombie's master plan, but stopped between 1959 and 1961 while Hay's department, led by Philip Andrews, revised its plans and designed a new main entrance facing Jameson Street. This reflected the westwards reorientation of the city centre as Abercrombie's plans for a northwards extension were abandoned. The new store included the Skyline Ballroom under a shell concrete roof, featuring two ceramic murals by Alan Boyson. The new facade was given even greater prominence with a still larger mural by Boyson, formed of 1,061,775 glass tesserae on a 66ft x 64ft (20m x 19.5m) concave concrete screen, in muted greens, blues and browns at the behest of the city planners. It depicts three stylised trawlers, whose masts spell out 'HULL', with the motto *RES PER INDUSTRIAM PROSPERAE* ('Things by Industry Prosper').

Boyson was the son of a Co-op manager, who had assisted Andrews's career by recommending him to the CWS, and the families were good friends. Boyson had trained as a ceramicist in Manchester and London, but so large were the Hull murals that they were executed in glass.

The Co-op closed the store as early as 1969, and it was occupied by British Home Stores from 1970 to 2016. The mural was threatened with demolition before it was listed in 2019, and its future remains uncertain.

Bhs
Bhs

EGG STORES

4–6 Stamford Hill, Stoke Newington, London
1967–69; Ervin Katona

The Egg Stores opened in 1948 (some sources say 1951) and did originally sell mainly eggs. It was taken over in 1967 by the Friedlander family and now serves the local Hassidic and wider Jewish communities as a 'one-stop shop for all things Kosher', from magazines and party stationery to imported foodstuffs and sweets. Mrs Erica Friedlander herself specialises in 13 varieties of schmaltz herring. The stores suffered a fire in 2012 but the blue 1960s frontage remains a local landmark.

The stylistic freedoms of mid-century modern, seen in fonts, colours and materials, lend themselves perfectly to shop fronts. They are ephemeral, however, and also hard to research. Yet while there are no surviving plans for the Egg Stores, there are for the building next door – and actually the two addresses are a single block of flats above the shops. Sam Stoller, fish specialist at No.8, and Monk Brothers, greengrocer at No.10, once had similar shop fronts. The lettering was a little smaller but there were the same speckled black mosaic risers (which survive) and blue glass fascias (which do not); that of the Egg Stores with its heavy 1960s lettering is now precious. The Jewish architect Ervin Katona emigrated from Czechoslovakia in 1938. In the late 1940s he developed the Orlit system widely used for prefabricated houses and flats; their big concrete panels and brick end walls are very distinctive, and these flats of brick and curtain-wall panels are an update of the idiom, if one rather out of time by 1969.

EGG STORES

BURBIDGE BAR
GYMS
JOIN NOW
BELLA ITALIA

ENTERTAINMENT

ODEON

ODEON CINEMA

Foregate Street, Worcester
1938–50; Robert Bullivant of Harry Weedon & Partners

Construction of a new cinema for Odeon opposite Worcester Foregate station was halted by the Second World War and passed to the Ministry of Aircraft Production, who cut a hole in a side wall so that the building could be used for storage. Robert Bullivant, who had designed many of the iconic Art Deco Odeons before the war as an assistant and later a partner to Harry Weedon, made revisions to his scheme before work recommenced. Construction in 1949 was specially allowed because the carcass was complete and materials were in place. But the original owner, commemorated in the name (later said to stand for Oscar Deutsch Entertains Our Nation), had died aged only 48 and the company passed to J. Arthur Rank, an enterprising Methodist who saw cinema exhibition as a means of reviving the British filmmaking industry. Money and materials were tight.

The cinema opened in January 1950 with 1,674 seats, only 14 fewer than planned in 1939. But the facade looked very different, with rolling curves to the walls and projecting roof rather than hard corners. The upswept canopy was designed to be crossed by neon bands, corresponding to the blue bands found today. There are no mouldings to the columns – a giant order reduced to its most minimal fundamentals. Below, the double entrance doors were set back, with shops to either side. The rest of the facade is almost blind, save for just two small windows, relieved by a quilted pattern of brick diapers. The cinema is now a seven-screen complex.

QUEEN ELIZABETH STADIUM

Donkey Lane, Enfield, Greater London
1939–53; Alec Mawson and successors
Listed grade II

Enfield Playing Fields were laid out at Bury Farm in 1936 by the borough council, funded by the King George V charity established to create recreation grounds in his memory. A lido opened, but war intervened before a planned athletics stadium could be built at its furthest end, and its architect Alec Mawson died in 1950 before materials became available to resume the project. Here, then, is a building that genuinely spans the war.

Spoil from the nearby Carterhatch refuse depot was used to create banking round the track, and the first Women's Southern Counties AAA meeting was held in September 1953. Enfield Council contributed £50 for the opening of the concrete grandstand and its crowning glory, the café on top of the changing rooms and offices. The style is moderne, ship-like yet featuring simplified curves and horizontal bars to the French windows that open on to the upper terrace with its sheltered seating. The tiled interior is reached from an oval entrance hall via an open staircase, also oval in shape and with a steel balustrade. Most telling is the circular funnel at its end, on which is painted the single word 'CAFE'. It would have disturbed the building's clean lines to add the accent.

The stadium, given its present name in 1977, closed in 2008 and lay derelict until in 2011 it was restored by Enfield Town Football Club, England's first club wholly owned by its supporters. The principal areas were lovingly restored as the clubhouse, and Tottenham Hotspur provided the first opposition.

CAFE
OUR NEXT HOME GAME
Saturday
14th
March
ENFIELD TOWN FC
VS
WORTHING
ENFIELD TOWN FC
WARNING

freedom
church
Church meets here

FORMER ODEON CINEMA

Bath Street, St Helier, Jersey
1948–52; T.P. Bennett & Son
Listed grade 1

No government licences were needed for the Channel Islands after the Second World War. J. Arthur Rank was thus free to build the first newly designed cinema in Britain after the war. It must have been a cheery sight following Jersey's occupation by German forces and a symbol of its rapid post-war revival.

St Helier followed the simplified style set by the Odeon at Worcester, with a central entrance and large window defined by piers set within an acreage of blank walling, here of combed render in a chequerboard pattern. A pattern resembling snooker balls highlights the windows. Local planners ordered the entrance to be set on a side street, though the 'Odeon' signage was on the main road.

Features in the upper and lower foyers were defined by coved lighting and pillars to the entrance and concession stands. The auditorium, later subdivided, was still simpler, with gentle curves and an arched opening instead of a formal proscenium, patchwork patterning resembling a jigsaw design and saucer-like hanging lights. Grey rather than black masking caused a stir in the film industry. The cinema opened on Whit Monday, 2 June 1952, with personal appearances by Margaret Rutherford, Kay Kendall and Anthony Steel.

Odeon subdivided the cinema in 1980 and again in 1989. It then built a multiplex elsewhere in the town and closed the Bath Street building in 2004. The planner Mark Price and I helped local activists fight off an application to demolish the cinema in 2011 and it became a church.

DEAL PIER

Deal, Kent

1954–57; William Halcrow & Partners, engineers

Deal is the austerity pier – no frills, just a gawky charm in its angled pairs of concrete piers and bus station entrance. Four shelters, set regimentally along its slender stem, offer a little protection to anglers. Yet this very minimalism imparts a rare elemental quality.

Deal has no harbour; its waters, where the North Sea and English Channel meet, are sheltered by the Goodwin Sands and boats were hauled up the shingle beach. John Rennie erected a timber pier in 1838, but it was never completed and was washed away in 1857. Eugenius Birch, the specialist engineer, built a replacement in 1863 that included a reading room and salt baths. In January 1940 the damaged 350-ton Dutch ship *Nora*, being towed towards the town, drifted against the pier and destroyed a quarter of it. Winston Churchill ordered the demolition of the rest to allow coastal guns a clear line of sight.

The new pier, 1,026ft (313m) long and costing £218,441, was opened by the Duke of Edinburgh in November 1957. The *Queen of the Channel*, operating day excursions to Calais, called until 1966. Jon Buck's *Embracing the Sea*, a sculpture as robust as the pier is skeletal, has stood by the entrance since 1998. A café at the sea end by the sensitive architect Niall McLaughlin was added in 2008 following a competition, its timber and glass structure bare-boned as befits its setting. The pier was restored in 2017–19 to celebrate its diamond jubilee, with a new clock at its entrance.

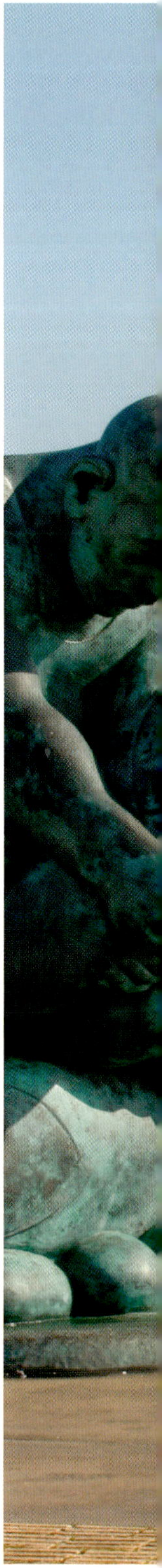

NO DOGS
CYCLES
OPEN
CCTV

NEVER
TURN
BACK
CLOSED
NO
BALL GAMES
ON GRASS
THANK YOU

NEVER TURN BACK

Manor Road, Caister-on-Sea, Norfolk
1956; A.W. Ecclestone
Listed grade II

Post-war pubs usually had a domestic look, and most have been heavily altered. A rare exception is the Never Turn Back, built to replace the Manor House Hotel, which was washed away by the sea in 1940 before the construction of Caister's sea wall. The first plans named the new pub as the Manor House, but then the name was changed to commemorate a nearby lifeboat tragedy in 1901. James Henry Haylett, the 78-year-old assistant coxswain, who helped rescue the only three survivors, explained to the subsequent inquest that 'Caister men never turn back' when setting out on a rescue mission, and the phrase became a lasting motto. The pub was officially opened in July 1957.

A 1930s cottage was adapted to provide accommodation for the landlord of the new pub, saving money and allowing it to assume its distinctive bungalow form and flexible internal plan. The architect to Lacons Brewery, A.W. 'Billy' Ecclestone, was fascinated by local history and archaeology, which may explain the vernacular brickwork and cobblestone. He also loved decorative tiles, following his early mentor J.W. Cockrill, the inventor of the Cockrill-Doulton patent tile. The bars occupy a single-storey rectangle, glazed on three sides, with double doors and verandas. The original bar fronts are thought to survive behind the present fixings of dark timber. To the south is a two-storey tower concealing the lavatories and boiler house, with tiles depicting the Lacons falcon and a lifeboat. The over-scaled name signs were originally picked out in blue neon and now have black backgrounds.

BELGRADE THEATRE

Belgrade Square, Coventry
1956–58; Coventry City Architect's Department, project architect Kenneth King
Listed grade II

The Belgrade was Britain's first post-war repertory theatre, and the first by a local authority following legislation in 1948. It was an important element of chief architect Donald Gibson's plan for the city, carried forward by his successor Arthur Ling, with Kenneth King becoming a theatre specialist. In an updating of repertory theatre's community tradition designed to combat the rise of television, there were 21 bedsits for resident actors, alongside workshops where the Belgrade's in-house productions were designed.

The main elevation, of Portland stone with double-height glazing, resembles that of Malmö's pioneering Stadsteater of 1932–44 and Mannheim's grandiose Nationaltheater of 1953–57. The foyer was decorated with delicate murals by Martin Froy and pendant lights by Bernard Shottlander.

The auditorium has a single gallery over shallow rear stalls, with a conventional proscenium stage (since extended). There were six stepped boxes either side, reminiscent of those at the Royal Festival Hall, now reduced to four with some used for lighting. The name commemorates President Tito, who made a gift of beech wood when visiting Coventry in 1953. The lengths were too short, so Yugoslavian timber can be found in local council housing while the theatre used West African hardwoods moulded into curves to give excellent acoustics.
A representation of Belgrade, created in concrete by Jim Brown from a 17th-century print, enlivens this elevation.

CAMERA PRINCIPIS

Kardomah

KARDOMAH CAFÉ

Portland Street, Swansea
1957, architect unknown

There was originally a chain of Kardomah cafés, named for a brand of tea first served at the Liverpool Colonial Exhibition of 1887 which was later applied to more teas, coffees and coffee houses. Branches in London and Manchester were by Sir Misha Black, the noted interior designer who worked on the Festival of Britain. Until it was bombed in 1941 the Swansea branch was at No.13 Castle Street, where a group met to discuss the latest in art, science and popular culture; these 'Kardomah boys' included Dylan Thomas, then working as a journalist on the *Evening Post* across the road.

This history has detracted from the living beauty of the replacement Kardomah Café. As the chain began to break up, in 1970 the Swansea branch was taken over by Pietro and Cathy Luporini, who decided not to update it, and it is now run by their son Marcus as a rare piece of retro chic in a city that has neglected its post-war heritage. Outside the columns and fascia are in yellow and gold mosaic above stone risers, with oval glass to the swinging doors on the corner set behind terrazzo flooring. The interior retains more mosaic, along with plywood panelling inset with reliefs in red and gold. The furniture, also original, includes unique tables with patterned Formica tops. Lines of indoor plants are another post-war feature, as is the chequerboard-tiled floor and extended staircase balusters. The award-winning café has even featured in an episode of *Doctor Who*.

MORELLI'S

Victoria Parade, Broadstairs, Kent
1957–58 onwards, architect unknown

Britain's first machines for making ice cream appeared in 1843, thanks to more regular ice shipments from Norway that were stored in huge pits, notably by Carlo Gatti at King's Cross. However, it was when refrigeration made ice cream more widely available that hundreds of Italian families emigrated to open parlours here. The Knickerbocker Glory appeared on a Lyon's Corner House menu in the 1920s. Soft-serve machines followed in the late 1930s, but it was in the 1950s that these appeared alongside Gaggia coffee machines in a new wave of seaside parlours.

The Kent resorts have the greatest concentration of surviving emporia. Morelli's is the most famous, first opened in 1932 but expanded and rebuilt in 1957–58. The winged chrome canopy resembles a giant Buick fender, tamed by ice cream cones to either side. Inside is sugar-almond pink – from the tentacles of ceiling plaster that once concealed cove lighting to the padded boudoir counter front. Amid later remodelling, wicker chairs impart a touch of class alongside a soda fountain and jukebox; even the soft-scoop machine is pink.

Broadstairs also has Chiappini's, less elaborate but delicious, while Ramsgate boasts Sorbetto, formerly Pelosi's, its interior as green as Morelli's is pink. My favourite is the Deal Beach Parlour, an authentic facade from the early 1960s (save for the doors), with blue mosaic under a zigzag chrome fascia, off-sales hatch and display window. For the stay-at-homes, Dominic Facchino launched his Mr Whippy ice cream vans in Birmingham in 1958.

MORELLIS
Continental Coffee
Soda
ICE-CREAM
CREAM PARLOUR
ICE-CREAM

RIVOLI BALLROOM

Brockley Road, Crofton Park, London
1958–59; converted by Leonard Tomlin
Listed grade II

From the street this modest building is indistinguishable from the many thousands of small cinemas. Yet the Crofton Park Palace, built in 1913 by Henley Attwater and remodelled in 1931, found a glamorous new use in 1959 as a ballroom.

This was the era of American jive and swing bands, as the Lindy hop and jitterbug gave way to new dances inspired by rock and roll, alongside the continued popularity of waltzes and foxtrots. A local businessman and dancing devotee, Leonard Tomlin, bought the cinema in 1957 and, over two years, inserted a luxuriant and exotic decorative scheme that was a homespun, updated version of the upmarket Art Deco ballrooms of the 1920s. Behind a timber-panelled foyer, the main ballroom retains a segmental-arched ceiling immediately recognisable as that of a 1913 cinema, but beneath it Tomlin installed a sprung dance floor of Canadian maple and clad the walls in red velour within the older plaster panels. A viewing area has red columns and quilting. Much of the effect comes from French chandeliers and Chinese lanterns. The ballroom is flanked by two narrow bars, including a members' bar added in 1960, one lined with leatherette seating and lit with saucer-shaped rococo lanterns, the other with a curved bar front of padded leather. The aesthetic is kitsch and flamboyant. The building is virtually unaltered and still in use as a dance hall, regularly seen in films, videos and on television.

BOSCOMBE PIER

Undercliff Drive, Bournemouth

1958–62; John Burton, Bournemouth Borough Engineer's Department

Listed grade II

The Boscombe Pier Company was formed in 1886 and a pier built in 1888–89, mainly as a landing point for pleasure boats. It was not originally successful and Bournemouth Corporation took over in 1904. It erected buildings at the pier head and 'neck', respectively the sea and landward ends.

The pier was rebuilt after wartime breaching, with new buildings. In 1961 a restaurant and Mermaid Theatre were built at the pier head, thought to be by Elisabeth Scott, who had returned to her home town after designing the Shakespeare Memorial Theatre. The theatre opened as a roller-skating rink and in 1965 became an arcade; never commercially successful, it was demolished in 2008. What survives is the simple yet striking boomerang entrance at the neck, a floating concrete canopy supported on four posts. There were originally just two kiosks and lavatories, with glazed screens and seating at either end; two more kiosks were soon added to either side of the originals, their timber facades bookended in cream tiles. Blue tiles face the sea, and the supporting concrete structure is faced in craggy natural stone – the balance of rough and smooth so important to mid-century design. It is a design of verve and vivacity, symbolising the golden age of the British seaside resort in the 1950s and an expression of sun, fun and ice cream. A £2.4 million restoration was completed in 2008.

REEFSIDE STORES

BAR
ZIP BASE
PierZip

PIER THEATRE

Bournemouth

1959–60; Elisabeth Scott of Bournemouth Borough Architect's Department

The Pier Theatre consciously resembles a paddle steamer heading out to sea, with a glazed captain's nest at the back of the fly tower. The hall itself is a simple structure lined in timber and braced externally, but to the rear the circular café-bar features a remarkable coffered shallow dome engineered to require no additional support. The theatre closed in 2013 and is now an activity centre, but the structure survives well.

Elisabeth Scott (1898–1972) was born in Bournemouth and studied at the Redmoor School on Canford Cliffs before entering the Architectural Association just two years after it began admitting women students. In 1928 she became the first woman to win a prestigious competition in Britain, that to rebuild the Shakespeare Memorial Theatre at Stratford-upon-Avon, completed in 1932 in a style that married contemporary Dutch, classical and Art Deco styles. Having formed a partnership with Maurice Chesterton and John Shepherd to redesign and erect the theatre, she went on to design the Marie Curie Hospital at Swiss Cottage (1929–30), destroyed in the Second World War, the Fawcett Building at Newnham College, Cambridge (1938), to house its growing number of women students, and Northallerton Senior School, North Yorkshire (1938–41). She briefly married, in 1936, her sister-in-law's brother, George Richards, a bankrupt, and returned to Bournemouth in the war. She continued working, first for A.J. Seal & Partners and then for Bournemouth Borough Council, designing halls for both Bournemouth and Boscombe piers. Scott and the Pier Theatre feature in the current British passport.

CLARENCE PIER

Southsea, Hampshire
1959–61; A.E. Cogswell and R. Lewis Reynish

One of Britain's biggest post-war pier structures was a café and ballroom at Clarence Pier, a concession to the fast food and funfair frolics of the seaside kept at arms' length from suburban Southsea. The last important work by the architects who gave the area its distinctive, characterful public houses, Clarence Pier's blue and yellow curtain walling and a golden crown to the central 60ft (18.3m) tower exude an ill-disciplined panache, enforced by a spiky butterfly roof in a secondary tower to the west. There was originally a double-height restaurant and a ballroom where dance bands played through the 1960s. It enjoyed a brief revival in 1980 – Wayne County and Alternative TV performed – but is now an amusement park and adventure playground.

The Clarence Pier is less a pier than a jetty, broader than it is long, built in 1861 for steamer services to the Isle of Wight. It was named for Lord FitzClarence, military governor of Portsmouth and one of William IV's illegitimate sons. An assembly hall was added in 1871, remodelled in 1932, and in 1882 the Prince and Princess of Wales opened an octagonal concert pavilion, where Adelina Patti gave the first recital.

The pier was destroyed on 10 January 1941. The substructure was rebuilt in 1953 and a new pub, the Seahorses, added to the west in 1958. However, the new pavilion – its circular floret surely a nod to the old pavilion – was not opened until the centenary of the original pier on 1 June 1961.

SOFT-PLAY
GOLDEN HORSESHOE
50' On Right Upstairs
WIMPY
Open
Every Day
All Year

FAIRFIELD HALLS
COACHES ONLY

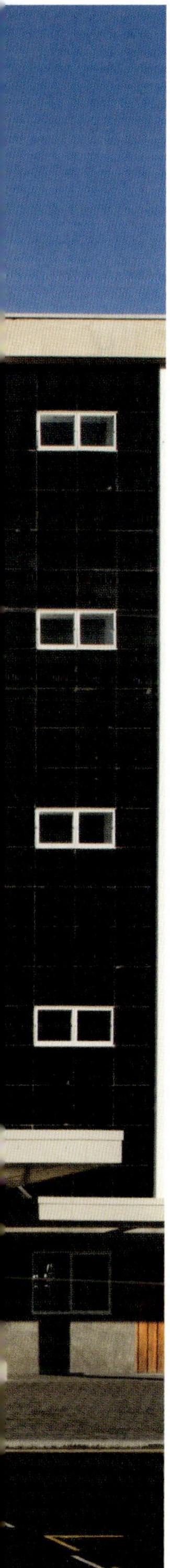

FAIRFIELD HALLS

Park Lane, Croydon
1960–62; Robert Atkinson & Partners

That there was only one concert hall built in Britain between 1950 and 1967 reflects a decline in demand for live music, which was blamed on the advent of the long-playing record. The building of the Fairfield Halls coincided with the demolition of the Davis, one of the largest and most lavish Art Deco cinemas, which had become a centre for theatre, opera and concerts as well as traditional cinema-variety. It is to the county borough's credit that it saw a need for a new type of entertainment centre to fill the gap, funded by leases to commercial developers elsewhere on the former goods yard it had purchased in the 1930s.

In 1960 Croydon commissioned the unique complex from Robert Atkinson & Partners, who had remained its architects after Atkinson's death in 1952. Its form remains indebted to the Festival Hall in its plan, with a large ground-floor foyer under the main hall, and in its external treatment of Portland stone and contrasting concrete panels. Structurally separate to aid the acoustics by Hope Bagenal, the last work by this important pioneer, the main hall was designed to seat 1,900 people; intended primarily for concerts, it also had facilities for films, conferences and wrestling matches. It is flanked by a flat-floored ballroom and the small Ashcroft Theatre, intended for plays and chamber music, and named for Dame Peggy, born locally. The building was carefully restored in 2015–19 by Mica Architects, who cleaned the facades and reinstated original features.

SPORTS PAVILION, GEOFFREY HUGHES MEMORIAL GROUND

Mather Avenue, Allerton, Liverpool
1961–63; Gerald Beech
Listed grade II

Gerald Beech (1921–2013) studied at Liverpool School of Architecture and taught there from 1948 into the 1980s, while running a small private practice. He was thus on hand to design the university's sports pavilion. He also personifies the most delicate modernism of the years around 1960, and whether a glass box was the natural choice for what it called 'a post-rugger bottle party' was questioned by the *Architects' Journal*. Yet, somehow, the pavilion has survived. This little block is remarkable for its continuous glazing, extending round the corners and set within delicate steel supports – though a recent adaptation as offices has led to partitions being introduced that have compromised the transparency of the upper storeys. Now you have to look more closely at the details to see just how good they are. The building rightly won a Civic Trust Award in 1963.

The grounds of Wyncote House were given to Liverpool University in 1922, and were always intended to be used for sports, though it was developed with pitches and a running track only in 1957. The tennis courts alongside the pavilion are more recent. The central three-storey block is linked to changing rooms and stores on one side, and to concrete terracing on the other, which serves as a grandstand to the adjoining rugby and cricket pitches. The buildings are picturesquely set beside a pond and trees, which mask the bulk of the ground-hugging changing rooms, linked by a bridge at first-floor level to the main pavilion.

OF STUDENTS
IN FRANCE
RECEIVED
AWARD IN
COMPLETION

Except
local buses
and taxis
Bigbelly

TRANSPORT

LOUGHTON STATION

Station Approach, Loughton, Essex
1939–40; John Murray Easton of Stanley Hall, Easton & Robertson
Listed grade II

London's Central Line was set to be extended in 1935, to the east taking over the former Great Eastern Railway line to Ongar, and to the west the Great Western Railway line to West Ruislip. Work halted in 1940 but not before one station was completed, commissioned by the London and North Eastern Railway (who chose the architects) on behalf of London Transport. The LNER instructed John Murray Easton to give the station an individual quality while conforming to the recognisable style established by Charles Holden. The brick is a little paler than Holden's, the forms simpler and the finishes more austere, but the light fittings are of bronze. The station opened in April 1940 although some features, including soundproofing tiles in the ceiling of the booking hall, were never installed. Offices and a mess room – part of which is now a public café – were set in a wing to the side. The most distinctive features are perhaps the kidney-shaped platform canopies that have the look of being coated in whipped ice cream. Timber platform benches with roundel backs, roundels in bronze handrails around the stairwells, the clock and poster boards all survive from 1940. The Central Line took over services in 1948.

Loughton was extensively developed by the London County Council after 1945, transforming the middle-class commuter town with new estates. Work also resumed on the Central Line, but it was to the west, with White City and especially Hanger Lane stations, that a new modern style emerged.

UNDERGROUND
LOUGHTON STATION
No parking

NEWBURY PARK BUS STATION

Eastern Avenue, Ilford, Greater London
1947–49; Oliver Hill
Listed grade II

Frank Pick, London Transport's design patron, was chairman of the Council of Art and Industry and first commissioned Hill to design the British Pavilion for the Paris Exposition of 1937. That year he also invited Hill to rebuild Newbury Park Station, recognising its value as an interchange in the electrification of what became the Central Line. Hill produced a design very like what was eventually realised. However, the war intervened, and in 1947 only the bus station and a canteen were deemed essential works and thus secured a building licence. Hill planned a series of round buildings and a tall pylon as a new station, but this backdrop of contrasting curves for the bus station remained unbuilt. Instead a temporary ticket hall was erected, originally painted orange and violet-blue, which survives today.

The simplicity of Hill's bus station symbolises post-war austerity. It is a concrete barrel vault of painful thinness, cast on seven round-arched ribs and sheathed in copper. The primitive concrete construction, with no pre-stressing, indicates the work of an architect rather than engineer, and perhaps its pre-war origins. It was a popular winner of a Festival of Britain Merit Award in 1951, attracting more votes than any other building; the distinctive Poole Pottery blue plaque featuring Abram Games's logo faces the road. It is such a striking local landmark that it was quietly listed as early as 1981, in a re-survey of older Redbridge buildings, as a 1930s design. It was restored in 1994–95.

PEDESTRIANS TUNNEL
CYCLISTS TUNNEL
2.3 m
Warning CCTV cameras in operation
No smoking

TYNE PEDESTRIAN AND CYCLE TUNNELS

Between Bewicke Street, Howdon, and Tyne Street, Jarrow, Tyne and Wear
1947–51; Mott, Hay and Anderson
Listed grade II

Northumberland and Durham County Councils approved the building of three tunnels under the Tyne in 1937, one each for cars, cycles and pedestrians. These were postponed by the Second World War but were authorised in 1946 at a time when the government put other infrastructure works on hold. The road tunnel was duly delayed until 1961, but in 1947 work started on pedestrian and cycle tunnels to serve the thousands working in the shipyards either side of the Tyne. They were the North East's greatest single contribution to the Festival of Britain.

The tunnels look modest – particularly the circular entrance pavilions with concrete shell roofs resembling pith helmets – but below is a wealth of detail. The escalators, at 85ft (25.9m) still the longest in the world with wooden treads, are now static illuminated features. As at the St Anna's Tunnel, Antwerp (1931–3), there were also conventional lifts, in separate buildings. Both tunnels are 900ft (274.4m) long, but the cycle tunnel at 12ft 2in (3.7m) is imperceptibly wider than that for pedestrians at 10ft 6in (3.2m). Both have the same aquatic green and cream tiles from Carter & Co., some incorporating serif lettering – especially at the former county boundary at mid-point. A road tunnel finally opened in 1968, by which time most of the docks had closed and few people used the pedestrian tunnels. The twin tunnels closed for complete refurbishment in 2013–19 with new inclined lifts due to open in 2021.

BUS GARAGE

Lansdowne Way, Stockwell, London
1951–54; Adie, Button and Partners
Listed grade II*

As London's last trams were withdrawn in 1952, so garages were urgently needed for a new bus fleet. Where depots already existed steel was available, but on new sites resort had to be made to concrete and Lord Ashfield, outgoing chairman of London Transport, ordered an inspection of the pioneering shell roof at Wythenshawe Bus Garage in Manchester. An experiment was made at Peckham (demolished) before shells were adopted at Stockwell, a prestigious new garage for buses replacing the trams that had run through the Kingsway Subway and the largest in Britain. John Smith of A.E. Beer and Co. was the engineer. It is 194ft (59m) wide and 392ft (119.5m) long; within, ten two-hinged portal frames arch from 16ft (4.9m) to an impressive 39ft (11.9), and between them nine shell cylinders soar 53ft (16.2m) into clerestory roof lights. A giant beam ties the roof at springing level to resist horizontal forces and, for added strength, the reinforcement rods were welded – the building's greatest technical novelty is thus entirely hidden. Roof lights cut into the shells cast an even, ethereal glow, while looking down from the nearby tower blocks they resemble a shoal of leaping dolphins.

Some 200 buses can be garaged here, yet they are dwarfed by the roof. Shells were a timely innovation for the many new bus stations because they could bridge wide spans cheaply and without columns. There are smaller examples in Bournemouth, Chichester and Dublin, but Stockwell is the outstanding example.

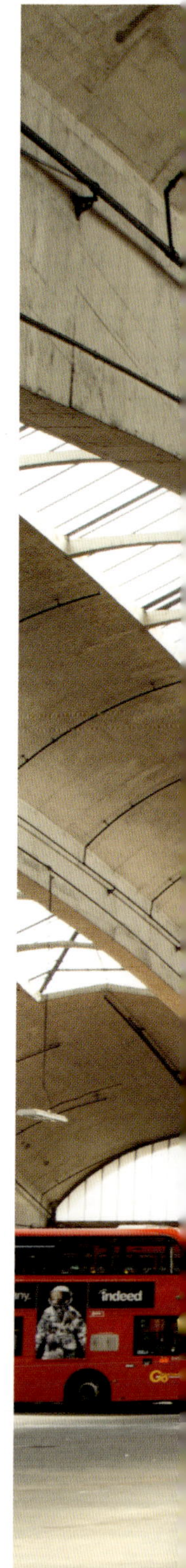

600

CANOPY TO FORMER PETROL STATION

A1, Markham Moor, Nottinghamshire
1960–61: Hugh Segar (Sam) Scorer
Listed grade II

The Lincoln-based architect Sam Scorer was fascinated by the possibilities of shell construction and in particular the work of Félix Candela, who gave several inspiring lectures in London in 1959. The same year Scorer designed a motor showroom in Lincoln – in return for a fast car – under a concrete 'hypar' roof. This was devised with the émigré Hungarian engineer Kálmán Hajnal-Kónyi as two pairs of handkerchief-like hyperbolic paraboloid forms divided by a roof light. The pair then collaborated on a petrol station for A.H. Turner on the Retford Bypass at Markham Moor, Nottinghamshire, which is seen by millions of motorists each year. Its canopy is a single hyperbolic paraboloid by Hajnal-Kónyi that reached 37ft 4in (11.4m) at its apex while the lowest points were only 5ft (1.5m) above the ground. In around 1980 a Happy Eater restaurant was inserted underneath, later rebranded as a Little Chef, but this lay derelict for over a decade until, in 2019, it was rebuilt by Starbucks.

Thin concrete shells were developed in Germany around 1920 as a means of achieving large spans with limited materials at little cost. Their strength is in their shape, for they carry loads by tensile forces in the plane of the shell rather than by the weight of their materials. The exiled architect turned engineer Félix Candela developed the anticlastic shell, with a double curvature, in Mexico around 1950. His favoured shape was the hyperbolic paraboloid for its strength and ease of shuttering, and this duly became Scorer's preferred form.

SEA TERMINAL

Douglas, Isle of Man
1961–65; Robert Bruce and C.J. Kneen of Davidson Marsh
in succession to T.H. Kennaugh

This glorious cake stand of a building gives a startling first impression of the Isle of Man for visitors by sea, a confection of the seaside at its best. It replaced a building of 1889 on the Victoria Pier, while also serving the Edward VIII Pier of 1936. Kennaugh was given the brief, but it was then passed to Davidson Marsh on the grounds that his practice was too small – curious, since he had recently designed the island's airport. The design follows the Isle of Man's three-legged symbol, the front legs a mirrored pair that frame a turning circle facing the shore. They radiate from a circular top-knot known locally as the Lemon Squeezer, formed of lightweight Omnia beams (concrete reinforced with a steel lattice structure) into which a concrete spike has been plunged. The blue and white panels are formed of mineralite, a mix of cement, granite and glass. The historian Gillian Darley has described the terminal as 'one of the happiest structures ever'.

The ground floor was planned as a waiting hall for 1,500 passengers, including a pleasant sun lounge and buffet. On the first floor was a viewing gallery, kitchens and offices, and the Lemon Squeezer housed the Crow's Nest Restaurant, closed in 2008. The upper floors are now all government offices.

With its long, sandy bay and 19th-century terraces of boarding houses, Douglas epitomised the British resort town. But its post-war revival ended spectacularly and catastrophically in 1973 with a conflagration at its leisure complex, Summerland, which killed 50 people.

WHSMITH
COSTA

PLACES OF WORSHIP

ALL SAINTS

Evelyn Avenue, Intake, Doncaster, South Yorkshire
1951–56; George G. Pace

George Pace was one of the few church architects to balance modernism with an older Arts and Crafts sensibility, but when he secured this suburban commission he had yet to find his mature style. The small windows that are typical of his churches still have a regular pattern, and there is a Scandinavian quality to the asymmetrical roof and fine brickwork that enlivens one of the first substantial churches built after the war. All Pace's major works are in the north or Wales, but he was originally from Croydon; this and other commissions from the Diocese of Sheffield enabled him to settle in York after serving there with the Royal Engineers.

All Saints was built on the foundations of a Romanesque church begun by Morris Thompson in 1938, but abandoned during the Second World War. Pace later embraced centralised church plans, but in 1950 he still believed in designing a liturgical east end, although he reorientated the plan he inherited so its compass points are actually the wrong way round. The result is a wide and very light church, with aisles of square columns widely separated, and a rippling blue ceiling that gives a good acoustic. Pace added more furnishings in 1956–57 and 1959, and the vicarage in 1958–59. The font is medieval, on a new shaft. The specialist church artist Harry Harvey added a mural in 1964 depicting Christ surrounded by apostles, evangelists and contemporary saints, blocky groups of figures pasted separately across the wall that are almost cartoon-like.

TRINITY UNITED REFORMED CHURCH

Unthank Road, Norwich
1954–56; Bernard Feilden with Edward Boardman & Son
Listed grade II

Like all Presbyterian churches, Trinity is a modest building. Yet it is more distinctive than most, thanks to its steep gable and a tower remarkable for its exaggerated entasis (the curve given to a tower or column to make it look straight to the eye). The tower has Scandinavian influences, best seen in its copper cupola. Feilden said he was also inspired by the 6th-century Sant'Apollinare Nuovo in Ravenna, seen when he was a serviceman in Italy and which has a similar juxtaposition of tower and gable.

The previous Trinity Church was destroyed in 1942, when its site was purchased by the council for redevelopment. Caley Mackintosh, from the congregation, had acquired the Unthank Road Baptist Chapel as a store and offered it for the new church. Its foundations determined the building's footprint and thence the plan of a first-floor church over a generous entrance area for meetings and gatherings. Internally the striking feature of the well preserved but traditional interior is the centralised steel roof structure clad in African hardwood, its triangular roof lights symbolising the Trinity and forming a cross over the main chandelier. Decoration is confined to the natural quality of the materials, save for small reliefs in the external panels of Westmorland slate.

Bernard Feilden (1919–2008) joined local architects Edward Boardman & Son in 1950. He was solely responsible for Trinity, and when Boardman refused him a partnership he set up his own practice. He was later knighted for his work as surveyor to Norwich Cathedral, York Minster and St Paul's Cathedral.

OTRE DAME DE FRANCE
ROMAN CATHOLIC CHURCH
5 LEICESTER PLACE

NOTRE DAME DE FRANCE

Leicester Place, London
1953–55; Hector Corfiato
Listed grade II

Notre Dame de France is a round church. This might be a foretaste of church planning in the 1960s, but is actually a historic accident since the church is built within the walls of Burford's Panorama, a diorama of 1793. Leicester Square was even then the centre of London entertainment and in 1865 the first French church served some 50,000 wine merchants, hoteliers, chefs, musicians and milliners (along with political refugees, sailors and prostitutes). It was bombed in November 1940, and its rebuilding was a government gesture led by Anthony Eden.

The new church owes most to the French Ambassador's cultural attaché, René Varin. He found the architect, a man of Greek descent trained in the French Beaux-Arts tradition who was head of London's Bartlett School of Architecture. Corfiato's distinctive classicism appears in the giant piers that support a gallery that doubles the church's capacity when needed. Below are parish rooms, used as a cinema, theatre and bar. However, it was Varin who found the artists whose work defines the building's look. He commissioned the sculpture of Our Lady (which is also a Madonna della Misericordia) over the entrance from Georges Saupique (1889–1961), master sculptor of Reims Cathedral, and the Aubusson tapestry behind the altar that dominates the interior. He then met the poet Jean Cocteau, who was receiving an honorary doctorate at Oxford University, and invited him to decorate a wall of the Lady Chapel, which includes his own self-portrait and was realised in one week in 1960.

CHRIST CHURCH

Frankpledge Road, Cheylesmore, Coventry
1954–58; Alfred H. Gardner
Listed grade II

The *Architects' Journal* derided Christ Church as 'pleasure gardens pastiche'. Gardner referenced the '"Prayer Book" church of the Wren period', but acknowledged having visited the Festival of Britain.

Thomas Rickman built the first Christ Church in central Coventry in 1830–32 around the surviving tower of the medieval Greyfriars' Church. It developed a powerful evangelical tradition, which survived the destruction of the church (but not the tower) in April 1941. The Diocesan Reorganisation Committee insisted that the replacement church be in the 1930s suburb of Cheylesmore. Moreover, Bishop Gorton (High Church and charismatic in his architectural tastes) rejected the church's evangelical design, which featured a pulpit against the east wall with a communion table and choir stalls in front of it. He imposed Gardner as architect.

What the congregation made of Gardner's design is not recorded. The disjointed exterior, with alternating panels of concrete and glass, gives little clue to the interior. The chequerboard patterning of the exterior is repeated inside, but how many churches are painted in lilac and gold? The light fittings are hanging birdcages inspired by that designed by R.D. Russell and Robert Goodden for the Lion and Unicorn Pavilion. The fenestration and the ceilings, particularly the lamella trusses of the church hall, derive from the same pavilion. The sculpture of Christ the Sower above the entrance porch, and inside wood carvings round the altar and clock are by John Skelton, the Coventry-born nephew of Eric Gill.

CATHEDRAL CHURCH OF ST MICHAEL

Priory Street, Coventry
1956–62; (Sir) Basil Spence & Partners
Listed grade I

Coventry's was the one cathedral damaged beyond repair in the Second World War, and its highly publicised destruction and rebuilding made it a symbol of Britain's post-war regeneration. Spence himself promoted the fund-raising campaign and became a household name. He won a competition in 1951 with a broadly Arts and Crafts design set at right angles and orientated north–south to the old ruins. For economy Spence recast the interior in 1955–56 using concrete block, with concrete-framed side chapels, after Arup had refined a lighter, faceted concrete vault. He redesigned the porch as a massive *porte cochère* linking the old and new buildings, conceiving a clear-glazed West Window etched with angels by John Hutton.

Spence was aware of liturgical changes but the reconstruction committee was conservative and instead he focused on securing the fine artworks for which the cathedral is renowned today, quickly commissioning them before others imposed economies, though this inhibited subsequent changes to the east end. They included Graham Sutherland's tapestry of Christ in Glory and ten windows by Lawrence Lee, Keith New and Geoffrey Clarke that established the Royal College of Art as a centre of glassmaking. John Piper's more individual baptistery window and Jacob Epstein's sculpture of St Michael quashing the devil followed in 1954–55.

On opening, the cathedral was described condescendingly as 'an uplifting place to take the girlfriend on a wet Sunday afternoon'. It is now recognised as one of Britain's great 1950s repositories of art and culture.

ST BONIFACE GERMAN CHURCH

Adler Street, Whitechapel, London
1959–60; Toni Hermanns
Listed grade II

How ironic that Britain's one Roman Catholic church for a German congregation should have been damaged by a Zeppelin attack in the First World War and then totally destroyed in 1940.

Whitechapel has had a German community since the 16th century, but large numbers of Roman Catholics settled only in the 1860s, when many migrants in transit to the United States instead stayed here, in business or as domestic servants. They converted a chapel in Adler Street, which collapsed in 1872 and was rebuilt.

Reconstruction in the 1950s was funded by the West German government and led by the parish priest, Father Felix Leushacke, who brought in the architect Toni Hermanns from his native Cleves/Kleve in the Rhineland. Donald Plaskett Marshall steered the scheme through the English authorities.

St Boniface is formed from a series of simple concrete portal frames, with brick as an external facing, and large areas of glass. Mosaic panels were used as permanent shuttering for the concrete tower, striking black crosses set against a background of yellow with touches of red. Inside there is a balcony with a fine organ installed in 1965, original fittings and benches. Dominant are the artworks, mostly from artists also from the Kleve area. Heribert Reul designed the font of dark-green marble and the dramatic sgraffito mural of coloured and textured plaster at the liturgical east end over the high altar. The only English artist was Reginald Lloyd, who created the west window.

ST PAUL

College Square, Harlow, Essex
1957–59; Humphrys and Hurst
Listed grade II

St Paul's is the most complete 1950s building in central Harlow. The Harvey Centre and the civic centre complex now obscure it, but it was intended to relate to the nearby water gardens. Frederick Gibberd suggested using brick to contrast with the town's secular buildings, giving it a sombre appearance save for zigzag decoration on the outdoor pulpit. The cross on the separate bell tower was copied from St Paul's Cathedral and the bells came from a bombed East End church, both a reminder of Harlow's links with London.

The interior, by contrast, is brilliantly light and colourful. The overall plan is traditional, with a long nave, save that the choir was placed in a gallery to one side, enabling the congregation to sit close to the altar. John Piper's mural dominates, depicting the Risen Christ at Emmaus and installed just ahead of his larger mural at the BBC Television Centre in Shepherd's Bush. It fills the east wall, the black mosaic forming a background to the semi-abstract figures. Their bright colours are repeated in the yellow ceiling and glass, blue ceiling and columns around the church, and in details amid the soft greys employed in the unusual altar furniture, organ and benches.

Derrick Humphrys and Reginald Hurst worked for N.F. Cachemaille-Day and J. Harold Gibbons before designing churches for the Diocese of Chelmsford, of which this is their masterpiece. Most of the design was made by Humphrys before his early death in 1958, with Hurst completing the fittings.

ST AIDAN, LEICESTER

St Oswalds Road, New Parks, Leicester
1958–59; Basil Spence & Partners

New Parks was Leicester's first post-war housing estate, begun in 1946. Church services were held in a community centre and then the church hall, dedicated in 1954 by the Bishop of Leicester from the roof of nearby flats. When in 1955 he learned of three low-cost parish churches being built by Basil Spence in Coventry to a common design, he invited the architect to design two churches for Leicester's housing estates. Only a hall was realised at St Hugh's, Eyres Monsell, but St Aidan's was duly built, and it is one of Spence's finest suburban churches.

St Aidan's follows the formula of Coventry, and has a simple, rectangular nave and sanctuary, a lofty campanile and a vicarage. Here, there is an additional wing of ancillary accommodation and a substantial cloister. The Coventry churches are entirely formed of concrete, but here it is used only for the frame, with brick infill cladding and timber ceilings. In 1956, however, Spence had visited Le Corbusier's chapel at Ronchamp and enthused about the spirituality of its 'atmosphere' and light.

A member of the Art Workers' Guild, Spence was keen to introduce works by artists alongside the fittings crafted by his assistants. The porch features a tile mural depicting scenes from the life of St Aidan by William Gordon. His first major tile commission, he had previously worked as a studio potter at Walton Pottery in Chesterfield and was responsible for the Carter & Co. abstract tile mural at Basildon Bus Station (now sadly lost).

ST AIDAN, ACTON

Old Oak Common Lane, East Acton, London
1960–61; John Newton of Burles, Newton & Partners

Father James Etherington, the first parish priest, met Newton when both worked in Southend-on-Sea, and revived the connection when he wanted a cheap church so as to have more money for art. This modest building holds the story of post-war religious art in Britain. It is dominated by Graham Sutherland's bright red hanging depicting Christ on the Cross, tortured here compared with the stillness of Coventry. Yet more intriguing are the lesser-known works that flank it, many by refugees. The Stations of the Cross, reliefs set in mosaic along each aisle, are by Arthur Fleischmann, who arrived from Slovakia via Bali in 1948. He was also a pioneer in etching Perspex, seen in panels depicting the Four Evangelists. At the east end of each aisle are triptychs by the Australian convert Roy de Maistre, depicting the Sacred Heart and Our Lady of Walsingham. The church has stained glass at ground level either side of the entrance and high up either side of the sanctuary. Both sets were designed by Pierre Fourmaintraux, a Frenchman who brought the *dalle de verre* technique to Britain.

The baptistry is particularly richly decorated. The large ceramic mural is by Adam Kossowski, who came from Poland in 1943 via a Soviet gulag and devoted himself to religious art in thanks, working with Fulham Pottery. The statues are by English artists, notably Kathleen Parbury, who sculpted the figure of St Aidan on the outside of the building; she had already designed a similar St Aidan at Lindisfarne, Northumberland.

TAUNTON DEANE CREMATORIUM

Wellington New Road, Taunton, Somerset
1961–63; Potter and Hare
Listed grade II

Crematoria are a shady building type, discreetly pushed to the architectural margins and little talked about. Yet no fewer than 75 were built in Britain between 1951 and 1959, with 72 more following in the 1960s as cremation rose from 15 to 60 per cent of all funerals. Most were designed and landscaped by local authority surveyors, with few attracting interest from the press.

The exception was at Taunton. Robert Potter was the leading church architect in the west of England, and visited crematoria across Europe before making his design. The result was a striking modern chapel, faced in local stone with an asymmetrical copper roof, its north front cranked to the north for added effect and with stained glass by Geoffrey Clarke set in aluminium. Behind, the crematorium is sunk into the side of the steep hill, save for the simple chimney. Across a covered roadway, the book of remembrance is housed in a separate circular chapel, then novel.

As significant was the setting, planned from 1956 by Peter Youngman, one of the first academic lecturers in landscape design. The hillside had been pasture, divided by deep ditches and wide hedges, most of which he retained, with trees making a backdrop to the chapel seen from the foot of the hill. In front he created a broad greensward and, at the entrance, a large plain cross in the manner of Gunnar Asplund's Woodland Cemetery at Stockholm, a major influence on the artfully natural style of cemeteries laid out in the post-war years.

SVENSKA SJÖMANSKYRKAN

SWEDISH SEAMEN'S MISSION

Lower Road, Rotherhithe, London
1964–66; Bent Jörgen Jörgensen with Elkington Smithers
Listed grade II

At a time when Swedish design was so influential and imitated, it is exciting to find a real Swedish building in London.

The Baltic timber trade established itself at the Surrey Commercial Docks in Rotherhithe, where missions from Norway, Finland and Sweden opened churches for visiting mariners in close proximity. The Swedish Mission Board took over a former library, which it extended in 1929 and substantially rebuilt after war damage, when Jörgensen designed a new frontage containing a servery and kitchen, library and recreational facilities, with staff flats and hostel accommodation above. Many fittings were shipped from central Sweden, including bespoke copper light fittings, ceiling panels and a *dalle de verre* entrance wall by Christer Sjögren of the Lindshammar glassworks. The copper signage to the front features an anchor and fish. Jörgensen also reordered and decorated the earlier church.

Bent Jörgen Jörgensen (1915–99) was a Danish-born architect who managed Arne Jacobsen's office in Copenhagen during the latter's wartime exile in Sweden. Jörgensen then settled at Växjö in central Sweden, designing churches in an area long associated with the Church of Sweden Abroad. The Swedish Lutheran church went through a period of liturgical reform, parallel to that in England, where the Småkyrkorörelsen or district church movement emphasised the building of community facilities within churches. The church in Rotherhithe closed in 2012 but the flats remain occupied.

FOOTNOTES

[1] Cara Greenberg, *Mid-Century Modern: Furniture of the 1950s*, New York, Thames and Hudson, 1984.

[2] 'The New Brutalism', *Architectural Design*, Vol.25, No.1, January 1955, p.1.

[3] Nikolaus Pevsner, *Pioneers of the Modern Movement*, London, Faber & Faber, 1936.

[4] Henry-Russell Hitchcock, *The International Style: Architecture since 1922*, New York, W.W. Norton & Company, 1932.

[5] F.R.S. Yorke, *The Modern House, London*, Architectural Press, 1934.

[6] Randall Evans, quoted in Alan Powers, *In the Line of Development, F.R.S. Yorke, E. Rosenberg and C.S. Mardall to YRM*, London, RIBA, p.18.

[7] Gerald Barry, *News Chronicle*, 14 September 1945.

[8] Ian Cox, *The South Bank Exhibition: A Guide to the Story it Tells*, London, HMSO, 1951, p.67.

[9] John Summerson, 'Lansbury', *New Statesman and Nation*, Vol.41, No.1058, 16 June 1951, p.679.

[10] *Architectural Review*, Vol.95, No.569, May 1944, p.113.

INDEX

Illustration references in italics

Aalto, Alvar 9, 18, 56
Abercrombie, Patrick 181, 210
Aberdeen, David du Roi 159
Adams, Robert 140
Adie, Button and Partners 252
All Saints, Intake, Doncaster 260, *261*
Allan, John *75*
Allen, Joseph S. 135
Alton East, Roehampton, London 118, *119*
aluminium 17–18
Amersham, Buckinghamshire, High and Over 6
Andrews, Philip 210
Angmering-on-Sea 8
Angus, Peggy 24, 197
Ansty Plum, Ansty, Wiltshire *94*, 95
Anthony, Monica and Muriel *47*
Antonietti, René 182
Architects' Collaborative 9
Architects' Journal 190, 242, 266
Architectural Association School of Architecture 8–9
Architectural Review 9, 11, 12, 14
architecture, training and education 5, 6, 8–9
Art Workers' Guild 274
Arts & Architecture 17
Arts Council 15
Arup, Ove 7, 88, 95, 139, 269
Asplund, Gunnar 9, 278
Atkinson, Fello 48
Attlee, Clement 11
Attwater, Henley 233
Avanti Architects 43

Backström & Reinius 118
Bagenal, Hope 241
Bailey & Lubetkin 117
Bailey, David 194
Bajó, Gyula 197
banks, National Provincial Bank, Plymouth 202, *203*
Banks, Olive 72
Bankside Power Station, Southwark, London 19, 178, *179*
Barbican 121
Bargood Estates 71
Barr, A.W. Cleeve 131
Barraclough, Frank 148
Barry, Gerald 11, 28
Basil Spence & Partners 18, 144, 269, 274
Basildon Bus Station 274
Bassett-Lowke, W.J. 6
Battersea Park 13, 28, *29*
Battye, Joe 51
Bauhaus, Dessau 6
Beale, John Elmes 189
Beales, Bournemouth *188*, 189
Beaulieu, Hampshire, Spence House 88, *89*
Beaux-Arts 5
Beech, Gerald *76*, 242
Behrens, Peter 6
Belgrade Theatre, Coventry 15, 226, *227*
Belluschi, Pietro 18
Belsky, Franta 197
Bergpolder flats, Rotterdam 110
Berlin, Free University 19
Bevan, Aneurin 9
Beveridge, William 9
Bevin Court, Islington, London *116*, 117
Bexhill, De La Warr Pavilion *7*
Bilsby, Leslie 56, 63
Bingham, Ken 206
'binuclear' dwellings 16
Birdham, West Sussex, Harbour Meadow 8, *42*, 43
Birds Bakery, Nottingham *208*, 209
Birkenhead, Wirral, Entwood *72*, *73*
Birmingham, Grosvenor House 190, *191*

Black, Misha 147, 185, 229
Blackett, Johnson 106
Bland, Kenneth 92
Boardman, Edward 262
Bonnington, Jack 17, 144
Booth, R. G. 102
Boots, Nottingham 18
Boscombe Pier, Bournemouth 234, *235*
Bournemouth
  Beales *188*, 189
  Boscombe Pier 234, *235*
  Pier Theatre *236*, 237
Bournemouth Borough Architect's Department 237
Bournemouth Borough Engineer's Department 234
Bousfield School, Kensington, London *142*, 143
'box-frames' *7*
Boyson, Alan 210
Brackenfell, Brampton, Cumbria 8, 38, *39*
Brady, John 80
Brampton, Cumbria, Brackenfell 8, 38, *39*
Brandlehow School, London 132, *133*
Brasted, Kent, Martins *46*, *47*
Breuer, Marcel
  'binuclear' dwellings 16
  British buildings *7*
  influence 51, 56, 67, 80
  international influences 8
Brewery Terrace, Stratford-upon-Avon *8*
brick bonds *5*
bricks 16
Brinkman, Johannes 5
Britain Can Make It exhibition 11
British Home Stores 15
British Iron and Steel Federation 10
Brixham, Devon, Parkham Wood House 80, *81*
Broadgate House, Coventry 182, *183*
Broadstairs, Kent
  Chiappini's 230
  Morelli's 230, *231*
Brockham, Surrey, High Bank 96, *97*
Brown, Capability 12
Brown, Jim 226
Brown, Michael 63, *79*
Bruce, Robert 256
Bruh, Max and Anne 84
Brutalism 19
BT Tower, London *168*, 169
Buck, Jon 222
Building 135
Bullivant, Robert 217
Bullock, Alan 152
bungalows 15
Bunshaft, Gordon 18, 148
Burles, Newton & Partners *277*
Burnham-on-Crouch, Essex, Royal Corinthian Yacht Club *7*
Burt Committee 10
Burton, John 234
bus garage, Stockwell, London 16, 252, *253*
bus stations
  Basildon 274
  Busáras, Dublin 16
  Newbury Park, Ilford 16, 248, *249*
Busáras, Dublin 16
Bushey, Hertfordshire, Palafitte *90*, 91
Butcher, G.A. 122
Butler, Reg 128
Buttle, Mr & Mrs 91

Cachemaille-Day, N.F. 273
Cadbury-Brown, H.T. 185
cafés, Kardomah Café, Swansea *228*, 229
Caister-on-Sea, Norfolk, Never Turn Back pub *224*, 225
Cambridge
  Crystallographic Data Centre 83
  Keelson *82*, 83
  Laslett House 64, *65*
  Raised Faculty Buildings, University *150*, 151
Cambridge Architectural Research Ltd 64
Candela, Félix 17, 255
Candilis–Josic–Woods 19
canopies 16
Carter & Co. 197, 251, 274
Carter, Kenneth 140
Carter's of Poole 24, 160, 186
'Case Study Houses' 17
Casson, Conder & Partners 151
Casson, Hugh 11, 12, 14, 151, 185
Castrol House, London 18
cathedrals
  Cathedral Church of St Michael, Coventry 88, *268*, 269
  Metropolitan Cathedral, Liverpool 174
Cedarwood, Woolton, Liverpool 76, *77*
Central Parade, Walthamstow 14, 160, *161*
Centre Point, London 17
Chamberlin, Powell and Bon 121, 143
Chert, St Lawrence, Isle of Wight *98*, 99
Chesterton, Maurice 237
Chiappini's, Broadstairs, Kent 230
Christ Church, Cheylesmore, Coventry 266, *267*
Chronowicz, Albin 206
churches *see also* cathedrals
  All Saints, Intake, Doncaster 260, *261*
  Christ Church, Cheylesmore, Coventry 266, *267*
  Notre Dame de France, London *264*, 265
  St Aidan, Acton, London *276*, *277*
  St Aidan, Leicester 274, *275*
  St Boniface German Church, Whitechapel, London *270*, *271*
  St Paul, Harlow, Essex *272*, 273
  Swedish Seaman's Mission, Rotherhithe, London *280*, 281
  Trinity United Reformed Church, Norwich 262, *263*
Churchill Gardens, Pimlico, London 5, 110, *111*
CIAM (Congrès Internationaux d'Architecture Moderne) 6, *7*
cinemas
  Odeon Cinema, St Helier, Jersey *220*, 221
  Odeon Cinema, Worcester *216*, 217
Circle 38
Clarence Pier, Southsea, Hampshire 238, *239*
Clarke, Geoffrey 185, 269, 278
Clarke Hall, Denis 24, 148
CLASP (Consortium of Local Authorities Special Programme) 17
classical buildings 5
Co-operative Store, Hull 210, *211*
Co-operative Wholesale Society 15, 210
Coates, Wells *7*, 8
Cockrill, J.W. 225
Cocteau, Jean 265
coffee bars 14
Cogswell, A.E. 238
collaboration 6, 9
colleges
  Hatfield Technical College, Hertfordshire 128, *129*
  Hull College 140, *141*
  Scarborough Technical College 18, 148, *149*
Collins, Henry 15
concrete, reinforced 5, 16, 17
Conder, Neville 151
Congrès Internationaux d'Architecture Moderne (CIAM) 6, *7*
Congress House, London *158*, 159
Connell, Amyas 6
Consortium of Local Authorities Special Programme (CLASP) 17
constructivism 6, 8, 12
Contemporary (Jackson) 4
Cook, Beryl 96
Coppin Dockray Architects 95
Coppin, Sandra 95
Corfiato, Hector 265
Cornish Unit housing 10
Cotton, Ballard and Blow 190, 205
Cotton, Jack 190
Coventry
  114 Kenilworth Road 52, *53*
  Belgrade Theatre 15, 226, *227*
  Broadgate House 182, *183*
  Cathedral Church of St Michael 88, *268*, 269
  Christ Church, Cheylesmore 266, *267*
  Lady Godiva sculpture 15
Coventry City Architect's Department 182, 226
Cox, Oliver 11, 118, 185
Crabtree, William 201
Crescent House, Golden Lane Estate, London 121
Crofton Gane 44
Crosby Library, Merseyside *172*, 173
Crosby, Theo 4
Crowe, Sylvia 14
Crowley, Mary 8, 131
Croydon, Fairfield Halls *240*, 241
Crystallographic Data Centre, Cambridge 83
Cullen, Gordon 12, 43
Cullenn, Gordon 132
The Culture of Cities (Mumford) 182
Cunliffe, Mitzi 186

Cunningham, Ivor 63, 71, *79*
curtain walling 4, 17–18, 140, 144, 148, 212, 238

Dannatt, Trevor 11, 64
Darley, Gillian 256
Davidge, W.R. 181
Davidson Marsh 256
Day, Robin 22
de Beer, Nico 95
de Courcy Fraser, Gerald 186
De Havilland 18
De La Warr Pavilion, Bexhill *7*
de Maistre, Roy *277*
de Stijl 6
Deal, Kent
Beach Parlour 230
Deal Pier 222, *223*
Denmark 5, 11, 18
Derek Lovejoy & Associates 92
Deutscher Werkbund 6
diaper patterns *5*
Dick, William Reid 15
district heating systems 110
Dome of Discovery, Festival of Britain 12, 18
Doncaster
All Saints, Intake 260, *261*
Swedish prefabs *10*
Dublin, Busáras 16
Dudok, Willem *5*
Dunton, Bedfordshire, village sign *30*, 31
Durham University, Durham *134*, 135

A.E. Beer and Co. 252
Easton & Robertson 128
Ecclestone, A.W. 225
Eden, Anthony 265
Edinburgh, Hunt and Steedman Houses *86*, 87
Edward Boardman & Son 262
Edwards, W.N. 68
Egg Stores, Stoke Newington, London 212, *213*
Ehrlich, Georg 131
Einzig, Susan 186
Ellesmere Port, Cheshire 13
Elson, G.M.D. 122
Emberton, Joseph *7*
Emett, Rowland 28
Enfield, Queen Elizabeth Stadium 218, *219*
Entenza, John 17
Entwood, Birkenhead, Wirral *72*, *73*
Epstein, Jacob 159, 186, 269
Erskine, Ralph 11
Etherington, James *277*
Evans, Randall 8
Experimental Building Department 10

factory-made housing 10
Fagus Factory, Alfeld, Hanover *5*
Fairfield Halls, Croydon *240*, 241
Farnley Hey, Farnley Tyas, West Yorkshire *50*, 51
Farnsworth, Edith 17
Fedeski, Henry 166
Feilden, Bernard 262
Festival of Britain 11–14
219 Oxford Street 32, *33*
Award for Merit plaque *15*
Britannia symbol 13
Dome of Discovery 12, 18
Lansbury Estate 24, *25–6*, 27
Pleasure Gardens 13, 28, *29*
Royal Festival Hall 13, 15, 18, 19, 22, *23*
sculptures 15, *34*, 35
village signs *30*, 31
Festival style 4
Fieldend, Strawberry Hill, Twickenham *78*, *79*
first principles 6
Fleischmann, Arthur *277*
Fourmaintraux, Pierre *277*
Frankfurt 5
Fraser, Sons & Geary 186
Frederick Gibberd and Partners 198
Free University, Berlin 19
Freyssinet, Eugene 194
Friedlander family 212
Froy, Martin 226
Fry, E. Maxwell *127*
Fuller, Buckminster 10
Fulton, John 147
Fullwell Cross Library, Barkingside, London 174, *175*
Gabo, Naum 8
Gaer Stelvio Estate, Newport, Wales 106, *107*
Gainsborough, Lincolnshire 13
Games, Abram 13, 27, 31, 248
Gandhi, Mahatma 136
Gardner, Alfred H. 266
Gardner, James 28
Geoffrey Hughs Memorial Ground, Allerton, Liverpool *242*, *243*
Gibberd, Frederick
Fullwell Cross Library, Barkingside 174
Gibberd House and Garden 60
Hull College 140
influence 13, 273
Lansbury Estate, market square and clock tower *27*
The Lawn, Mark Hall Moors 113
Market Square, Harlow 198
new towns 14
prefabrication 10
Gibberd House and Garden, Harlow, Essex 60, *61*
Gibberd, Patricia 60
Gibbons, J. Harold 273
Gibson, Donald 27, 182, 226
Giedion, Sigfried *7*, 9, 13
Gilbert and Hobson 99
Gilbert House, Pimlico, London 110
glass manufacturers 18
Gleadless Valley, Sheffield 122, *123*
Goddard, Herald and Joan 48
Golden Lane Estate, London *120*, 121
Goldfinger, Ernö 132
Gollins, Frank 148
Gollins, Melvin, Ward & Partners 18, 148
Goodden, Robert Y. 12, 185, 266
Goodman, S. Vincent 31
'Googie' style 4
Gordon, William 274
Grange Estate, Ealing, London 92, *93*
Graves, Sam 95
Gray, J. 122
Greaves, Walter 43
Green, David 5, 40, 114
Greenberg, Cara 4
Greenen, Wallace A. 189
Greenside School, London 132, *133*
Gropius Building, Impington Village College, Cambridgeshire *7*, 8, *126*, 127
Gropius, Walter
Architects' Collaborative 9
Bauhaus 6
Fagus Factory, Alteld, Hanover 5
Impington Village College, Cambridgeshire *7*, 127
Monico Café 190
packaged housing 10
silos 194
Grosvenor House, Birmingham 190, *191*
Gwynne, Patrick *75*, 84
Haddock, Koo 99
Hajnal-Kónyi, Kálmán 255
Halley Academy, London *138*, 139
Hallfield Estate, Paddington, London *108*, 109
Hammond, H.W. 181
Hammonds, Hull *180*, 181
Harbour Meadow, Birdham, West Sussex 8, *42*, 43
Harding, Valentine 8
Hardy Henrion, Daphne 35
Haringey Civic Centre, Wood Green, London *162*, 163
Harlow Art Trust 15
Harlow, Essex
Gibberd House and Garden 60, *61*
The Lawn, Mark Hall Moors *112*, 113
Market Square 198, *199*
St Paul *272*, 273
The Stow 14
Harper, Ross 52
Harry Weedon & Partners 217
Harvey, Bet 52
Harvey, Harry 260
Harvey, Robert 52
Haskell, Douglas 4
Hastings, Hubert de Cronin 12
Hatfield aircraft hangars 18
Hatfield Technical College, Hertfordshire 15, 128, *129*
Haward, Birkin 148
Hay, G.S. 210
Haylett, James Henry 225
Heinz, Hayes, Uxbridge 18
Henley-on-Thames, Oxfordshire, Past Field *74*, *75*
Hennebique 5
Henrion, F.H.K. 132
Henry Hope & Sons 18
Hepworth, Barbara 15, 128, 201
Hermanns, Toni 270
Herzog & de Meuron 178
Higgins, John and Beryl 96
High and Over, Amersham, Buckinghamshire 6
High Bank, Brockham, Surrey *96*, *97*
High Sunderland, Selkirk, Borders *58*, 59
Highpoint II, Highgate, London *7*
Hilary Taylor & Associates 28
Hill, D.E. 160
Hill, Oliver 248
Hills of West Bromwich 131
Hilversum 5
Hinchliffe, Ernest 17

Hitchcock, Henry-Russell *7*
Hodder, Stephen 152
Holborn Library, London 170
Holden, Charles 22, 246
Holden, Walter 202
Holloway, Anthony 15
Holliday, Clifford *197*
Holscher, Knud 152
Hornsey Library, Crouch End, London 170, *171*
Hoskin, Hugh 182
hostels, YMCA Indian Student Hostel, London 136, *137*
House & Garden 17
House & Home 4
'House of the Year' *76*
houses, design 15–16
Hove, East Sussex, Park Gate *70*, *71*
Howe, Jack 127
Hull
  Hammonds *180*, 181
  Hull College 140, *141*
  Three Ships Mural 210, *211*
Humphrys and Hurst 273
Humphrys, Derrick 273
Hunstanton School 17
Hunt House, Edinburgh *86*, *87*
Hurst, Reginald 273
Hutton, John 269
Huxley-Jones, T.B. 170

ice cream parlours 230, *231*
Ilford, Newbury Park bus station 16, 248, *249*
Imperial Chemicals 194
Impington Village College, Cambridgeshire *7*, 8, *126*, 127
International Publishing Corporation (IPC) 193
The International Style (Hitchcock & Johnson) *7*
Isle of Man, sea terminal, Douglas 256, *257*
Isle of Wight
  Chert, St Lawrence *98*, 99
  New House, Luccombe 44, *45*

Jackson & Greenen 189
Jackson, Alec Walter 189
Jackson, Gordon 189
Jackson, Lesley 4
Jacobsen, Arne 18, 19, 152, 163, 281
Jakobsen, Preben 63
James Cubitt and Partners 48
James, F. Norman 202
Jarrow, Tyne and Wear, pedestrian and cycle tunnels *250*, 251
Jarvis, G.F.S. 170
Jellicoe, Geoffrey 14, 156
Jersey, Odeon Cinema, St Helier *220*, 221
John Lewis & Partners 205
  Oxford Street, London *200*, 201
John Murray Easton 246
Johnson-Marshall, Stirrat 17, 131
Johnson, Philip *7*, *67*
Jörgensen, Bent Jörgen 281

Kahn, Louis *67*
Kardomah Café, Swansea *228*, 229
Katona, Ervin 212
Keelson, Cambridge *82*, 83
Kennard, Olga 83
Kennaugh, T.H. 256
Kenyon, Arthur 105
Kenyon, George W. 164
Kew, G.W. 160
Kidbrooke School, London *138*, 139
King, Cecil Harmsworth 193
King, Kenneth 226
kitchens 16
Klein, Bernat 59
Kneen, C.J. 256
Knight & Lee, Southsea, Hampshire *204*, 205
Knight, Jesse 205
Kossowski, Adam 277

Lambert, Maurice 185
Lancaster, Osbert 28
landscape design 14
Lansbury Estate 13, 14, *26*, *27*
Lansbury Lawrence School 24, *25*
Lasdun, Denys 109
Laslett House, Cambridge 64, *65*
Laslett, Peter 64
Lasswade, Lothian, Wilson House *66*, *67*
Lautner, John 4
The Lawn, Mark Hall Moors, Harlow, Essex *112*, 113
Le Corbusier
  influence 6, *7*, 44, 52, 80, 144, 274
  silos 194
  Weißenhofsiedlung, Stuttgart 6
Leamington Spa, Lillington Library 166, *167*
Ledeboer, Judith 14
Lee, Edward 205
Lee, George Henry *76*
Lee, Lawrence 269
legacy 19
Leicester
  22 Avenue Road 48, *49*
  St Aidan 274, *275*
Lescaze, William 9
Leushacke, Felix 270
Lever House, New York 18
Levitt, David 95
Lewis, David 186
Lewis, John Spedan 201
Lewis's Department Store, Liverpool 186, *187*
Ley, Frank 170
libraries
  Crosby Library, Merseyside *172*, 173
  Fullwell Cross Library, Barkingside 174, *175*
  Hornsey Library, Crouch End 170, *171*
  Lillington Library, Leamington Spa 166, *167*
Lillington Library, Leamington Spa 166, *167*
Ling, Arthur 226
Lion and Unicorn Pavilion, Festival of Britain 12
listing system 19
'Live Architecture' exhibition 13
Liverpool
  Cedarwood, Woolton 76, *77*
  Geoffrey Hughes Memorial Ground, Allerton 242, *243*
  Lewis's Department Store 186, *187*
  Liverpool University 5, 242, *243*
  Metropolitan Cathedral 174
  sugar silo 194, *195*
Llewelyn Davies, Richard 43
Lloyd, Reginald 270
LNER 246
Loddon New Town, Loddon, Norfolk 114, *115*
London
  Alton East, Roehampton 118, *119*
  Bankside Power Station, Southwark 19, 178, *179*
  Battersea Park 13, 28, *29*
  Beechworth Close, Hampstead Heath 84, *85*
  Bevin Court, Islington *116*, 117
  Bousfield School, Kensington *142*, 143
  Brandlehow School 132, *133*
  bus garage, Stockwell 16, *252*, *253*
  BT/Post Office Tower *168*, 169
  Castrol House 18
  Central Parade, Walthamstow 14, 16, 160, *161*
  Centre Point 17
  Churchill Gardens, Pimlico 5, 110, *111*
  Congress House *158*, 159
  Corner Heath, Blackheath *79*
  Egg Stores, Stoke Newington 212, *213*
  Festival of Britain 11–14
  Fieldend, Strawberry Hill, Twickenham *78*, 79
  Fullwell Cross Library, Barkingside 174, *175*
  Golden Lane Estate *120*, 121
  Grange Estate, Ealing 92, *93*
  Greenside School 132, *133*
  The Hall, Foxes Dale, Blackheath Park *62*, 63
  Hallfield Estate, Paddington *108*, 109
  Haringey Civic Centre, Wood Green *162*, 163
  Highpoint II, Highgate *7*
  Holborn Library 170
  Hornsey Library, Crouch End 170, *171*
  John Lewis & Partners, Oxford Street *200*, 201
  Kidbrooke School *138*, 139
  Lansbury Estate 13, 14, *26*, *27*
  Lansbury Lawrence School 24, *25*
  Leonard Manasseh's House *34*, 35
  Moro House, Blackheath Park 56, *57*
  Newbury Park bus station, Ilford 16, 248, *249*
  Notre Dame de France *264*, 265
  219 Oxford Street 32, *33*
  Persant Road 102, *103*
  Peter Jones 18
  Queen Elizabeth Stadium, Enfield 218, *219*
  Rivoli Ballroom, Crofton Park *232*, 233
  Royal Festival Hall 13, 15, 18, 19, 22, *23*
  Royal Lancaster Hotel 14
  St Aidan, Acton *276*, 277
  St Boniface German Church, Whitechapel 270, *271*

The Studio, Duke's Head Yard, Highgate 40, *41*
Swedish Seaman's Mission, Rotherhithe *280*, 281
Time and Life Building 14, *184*, 185
YMCA Indian Student Hostel, Camden 136, *137*
London County Council Architect's Department 18, 118
art commissions 15
London Transport 248, 252
London Underground 246, *247*
Loos, Adolf 5, 64
Loughton Station, Essex 246, *247*
Lubetkin, Berthold *7*, 22, 68, 109, 110, 117
Luporini, Pietro and Cathy 229
Lutyens, Edwin 159
Lyons, Eric 63, *71*, *79*

McCallum, Ian 47
McDowell, Connie 99
McGrath, Raymond 6
Mackenzie, Ian *76*
Mackintosh, Caley 262
McLaughlin, Niall 222
McWilliams, F.E. 144
Malmö, State Theatre (Stadsteater) 18, *19*
Mamourian House, Morpeth, Northumberland 68, *69*
Manasseh, Leonard 35, 185
Mardall, Cyril 105
Markham Moor, Nottinghamshire, petrol station canopy *254*, 255
MARS Group 11
Marshall, Donald Plaskett 270
Martin, Leslie 8, 18, 22, 38
Martin-Smith, Donald 122
Martins, Toys Hill, Brasted, Kent *46*, *47*
Mason, Ronald 173
Matthew, Robert 11, 22, 105
Mawson, Alec 218
May, Ernst 5, 40, 114
Meadows, Bernard 159
Melvin, James 148
Memorial Gardens, Walsall, West Midlands 156, *157*
Mendelsohn, Erich *7*, 194, 201
Merseyside
Crosby Library *172*, 173
Parker's house *54*, *55*
Metropolitan Cathedral, Liverpool 174
'Mi-Mo' 4
Miami Modern 4
Mica Architects 241
Mid-Century Modern: Furniture of the 1950s (Greenberg) 4
Mid-century Modernism 8–9
Mies van der Rohe, Ludwig 6, 17, 144, 148
Miles, George F. 202
Milles, Carl 9
Ministry for Education 17
Ministry of Aircraft Production 217
Ministry of Education 132
Ministry of Public Buildings and Works 169
Ministry of Works and Buildings 9
Mitchell, Frederick 170
Mitchell, William 15, 140
Moberly, Arthur 201
Modern Architecture Research (MARS) Group *7*
The Modern House (Yorke) *7*–8
Modernism 4–9, 19
modular buildings 17, 19
Møller, C.F. 128
Møller, Erik 163
Moore, Henry 15, 185
Morelli's, Broadstairs, Kent 230
Moro, Peter *7*, 8, 22, 43, 56, 64
Morpeth, Northumberland, Mamourian House 68, *69*
Morris & Steedman *87*
Morris, Henry 127
Morris, James *67*
Morris, William 5, 160
Morrison, Herbert 11
Morton, Alastair 38
motels 4
Mott, Hay and Anderson 251
Moya, Hidalgo 5, 12, *47*, 110
Mumford, Lewis 182

Nash, S.W. 160
National Provincial Bank, Plymouth 202, *203*
Neave, David 140
neo-modernism 19
Netherlands 5
Neutra, Richard 9
neutrality 18, 19
Never Turn Back, Caister-on-Sea, Norfolk *224*, 225
New Brutalism 4, 19
'New Empiricism' 4
New House, Luccombe, Isle of Wight 44, *45*
'New Humanism' 4
New, Keith 269
new towns 10, 14, 19
New Ways, Northampton 6
New York
Lever House 18
World's Fair 12
Newbury Park bus station, Ilford 16, 248, *249*
Newcastle upon Tyne, Civic Centre, Barras Bridge 164, *165*
Newingreen, Kent 4
Newport, Wales, Gaer Stelvio Estate 106, *107*
Newton, John *277*
Nicholson, Ben 38, 128
Niemeyer, Oscar 17
Norris, Dom Charles 166
Northampton
New Ways 6
St Matthew's 15
Norwich, Trinity United Reformed Church 262, *263*
Notre Dame de France, London *264*, 265
Nottingham
Birds Bakery *208*, 209
Boots 18
Nottinghamshire, CLASP system 17

Odeon Cinema, St Helier, Jersey *220*, 221
Odeon Cinema, Worcester *216*, 217
Odhams Press Hall, Watford, Hertfordshire *192*, 193
Odhams, William 193
offices, Grosvenor House, Birmingham 190
Orlit system 212
Oud, J.J.P. 5
Oulton Broad, Suffolk, Ultuna 48
Ove Arup and Partners 16, 139
Overshot, Oxford 8
Oxford
Overshot 8
St Catherine's College 19, 152, *153*

Pace, George G. 260
packaged housing 10
Page, Russell 28
Palafitte, Bushey, Hertfordshire *90*, 91
Pallot, Joyce 15
Palmer, Frederick Charles 202
Pannier Market, Plymouth 206, *207*
Parbury, Kathleen *277*
Park Gate, Hove, East Sussex *70*, *71*
Parker, J. Roy *55*
Parkham Wood House, Brixham, Devon 80, *81*
Pasmore, Victor 164
Past Field, Henley-on-Thames, Oxfordshire *74*, *75*
Paxton, D.R. 122
P.E. Gane 8
Pearn, C.H. Paul 206
Pelosi's, Ramsgate 230
Persant Road, Excalibur Estate, London 102, *103*
Pevsner, Nikolaus 5
Peter Jones, London 18
Pettiward, Roger 40
Pick, Frank 248
Pickles, Wilfred 132
picturesque movement 11–12
Pier Theatre, Bournemouth *236*, *237*
piers
Boscombe Pier, Bournemouth 234, *235*
Clarence Pier, Southsea 238, *239*
Deal Pier, Kent 222, *223*
Pike, Charles 139
Pilkington's 18
pilotis 6, 8, 18, 140, 156
Piper, John 28, 164, 269, 273
planning legislation 4
Plymouth
National Provincial Bank 202, *203*
Pannier Market 206, *207*
point blocks 92, 113, 118
Post Office Tower, London *168*, 169
Potter and Hare 278
Potter, Robert 278
Powell, Geoffry 121, 143
Powell, James 181
Powell, Philip 5, 12, *47*, 110
power stations 10
Bankside Power Station, Southwark 178, *179*
Powers, Alan 8
prefabrication 10, 19, 102, 105, 131, 132, 212
Price, Mark 221
printworks, Odhams Press Hall, Watford, Hertfordshire *192*, 193
Prizeman, John 91
projecting headers 5
public art 14–15
pubs, Never Turn Back, Caister-on-Sea, Norfolk *224*, 225
Purcell 152

Purdey, John 88

Queen Elizabeth Stadium, Enfield 218, *219*

Ramsgate, Pelosi's 230
Rand, Geoffrey *75*
Rank, J. Arthur 217, 221
rationing 9–10, 11
Rayner & Fedeski 166
Rebuilding Britain exhibition (RIBA) 10
Redington, Louis and Ursula *72*
Reilly, Charles 201
Reul, Heribert 270
Reynish, R. Lewis 238
RIBA 10
Richard Seifert & Partners 17
Richards, Ceri 147
Richards, James 24
Rigby, Roger 95
Rivoli Ballroom, Crofton Park, London *232*, 233
Robert Atkinson & Partners 151, 241
Robertson, Howard 128
Ronald Ward and Partners 32
roofs 5, 6, 8
Rosenauer, Michael 185
Rostas, Rachel 64
Rotterdam 5
Rowse, Eric A.A. 9
Royal College of Art 269
Royal Corinthian Yacht Club, Burnham-on-Crouch, Essex *7*
Royal Festival Hall, London 13, 15, 18, 19, 22, *23*
Royal Lancaster Hotel, London 14
Royal Society of Arts 11
Russell, Robert D. 12, 266
Ryder, Gorden 68

Saarinen, Eero 18
Saarinen, Swanson and Saarinen 18
Sachlichkeit 6
Salmon, Jack 32
Salmon, Liz and Tony *75*
Samuel, Edward 95
Samuel, Godfrey 8
Samuely, Felix 12, 128
Sansbury, Charles 164
Saupique, Georges 265
Sayers, John 163
Scarborough Technical College 18, 148, *149*
Schiedhelm, Manfred 19
schools
Bousfield School, London *142*, 143
Brandlehow School, London 132, *133*
Greenside School, London 132, *133*
Gropius Building, Impington Village College, Cambridgeshire *126*, 127
Hunstanton School 17
Kidbrooke School, London *138*, 139
Lansbury Lawrence School, London 24, *25*
steel frames 17
Templewood School *130*, 131
Scorer, Sam 255
Scott, Elisabeth 234, 237
Scott, Giles Gilbert 178
Scott, Michael 16
sculptures 14–15
sea terminal, Douglus, Isle of Man 256, *257*
Seal, Mervyn 80
Segal, Walter 9
Seidler, Harry 16
Selkirk, Borders, High Sunderland *58*, *59*
Sert, Josep Lluís *7*, 16
Shakespeare Memorial Theatre, Stratford-upon-Avon 237
Shand, Philip Morton 5
Shankland, Graeme 11, 118
Sheffield
Gleadless Valley, Sheffield 122, *123*
Sheffield University 18
Sheffield City Architect's Department 122
shell construction 16, 252, 255
Shepheard, Peter 197
Shepherd, John 237
Sheppard, Richard 148
Sherren, Brian C. 202
shops
Beales, Bournemouth *188*, 189
Birds Bakery, Nottingham *208*, 209
Co-operative Store, Hull 210, *211*
Egg Stores, Stoke Newington 212, *213*
Hammonds, Hull *180*, 181
John Lewis & Partners, Oxford Street *200*, 201
Knight & Lee, Southsea *204*, 205
Lewis's Department Store, Liverpool 186, *187*
Peter Jones, London 18
Shottlander, Bernard 226
Shulman, Julius 17
Silkin, Lewis 197
silos 16–17
sugar silo, Liverpool 194, *195*
Sir John Brown, A. E. Henson & Partners 163
Sitte, Camillo 198
Sjögren, Christer 281
Sjöström, Cyril 105
Skelton, John 266
Skidmore, Owings & Merrill 18
Skylon, Festival of Britain 12
Slater & Uren 201
Slater, Moberly, Uren and Pike 139
Smith, John 252
Smithers, Elkington 281
Smithson, Alison 17, 19, 95
Smithson, Peter 17, 19, 95
'Soft Brutalism' 4
Sørensen, Erik 64, 83
Souter, Alan E. 202
South Bank, London *see* Festival of Britain
Southampton University 18, 144, *145*
Southgate, F.G. 160
Southsea, Hampshire
Clarence Pier 238, *239*
Knight & Lee *204*, 205
Span Developments 63, 71, 79
Speight, Sadie 8, 38
Spence, Basil 88, 144, 269, 274
Spence House, Beaulieu, Hampshire 88, *89*
St Aidan, Acton, London *276*, 277
St Aidan, Leicester 274, *275*
St Boniface German Church, Whitechapel, London 270, *271*
St Catherine's College, University of Oxford 19, 152, *153*
St Paul, Harlow, Essex *272*, 273
stadiums, Queen Elizabeth Stadium, Enfield 218, *219*
Stanley Hall, Easton & Robertson 246
State Theatre (Stadsteater), Malmö 18, *19*
Steedman House, Edinburgh *86*, 87
Steedman, Robert 67, 87
steel frames 17
Stein, Clarence 197
Stephenson, Gordon 197
Stevenage Development Corporation 197
Stevenage town centre *196*, 197
Stirling, Hector J.W. 206
Stirling, James 151
Stjernstedt, Rosemary 118
Stockholm Exhibition 9, 12
Stockwell bus garage 16, 252, *253*
Stoddart, R.W. 27
Stratford-upon-Avon
Brewery Terrace *8*
Shakespeare Memorial Theatre 237
Strauss, Patricia 15
Stuttgart 6
subsidence 17
sugar silo, Liverpool 194, *195*
Sullivan House, Pimlico, London 110
Summerson, John 13
Sutherland, Graham 269
Svenska Trähus 105
Swansea, Kardomah Café *228*, 229
Swansea University *146*, 147
Sweden 5, 9, 10, 11, 18
'Swedish Grace' 5
Swedish prefabs, Marshland St James, Wisbech, Norfolk *104*, 105
Swedish Seaman's Mission, Rotherhithe, London *280*, 281

Tate & Lyle Engineer's Department 194
Tate Gallery 10
Tate Modern 19, 178
Taunton Deane Crematorium, Somerset 278, *279*
Tawse, George and Pauline 43
Tayler, Herbert 5, 40, 114
Tecton 109
Templewood School, Welwyn Garden City, Hertfordshire *130*, 131
temporary buildings 8, 9, 16
Temporary Housing Act 10
Tennant, Trevor 128, 182
Tew, Pat 131
Tewin, Hertfordshire 8
theatres
Belgrade Theatre, Coventry 15, 226, *227*
Pier Theatre, Bournemouth *236*, 237
Shakespeare Memorial Theatre, Stratford-upon Avon 237
State Theatre (Stadsteater), Malmö 18, *19*

This is Tomorrow exhibition 18
Thomas, Dewi-Prys *72, 76*
Thomas, Dylan 229
Thomas, Norman *147*
Thomas, Percy *147*
Thompson, Morris 260
Thompson, Peter 84
Three Ships Mural, Hull 210, *211*
timber housing 10
Time and Life Building, London 14, *184*, 185
'tin towns' 10
Tisdall, Hans 28
Tomlin, Leonard 233
'townscape' 12
Townsend, Geoffrey 63, *71*
T.P. Bennett & Son 181, 221
Trades Union Congress 159
Trinity United Reformed Church, Norwich 262, *263*
Truman, Hanbury, Buxton & Co *27*
Tubbs, Ralph 12, 136
Tucker, Victor 95
Tunley, A.N. 122
tunnels, Tyne pedestrian and cycle tunnels *250*, 251
Turner, A.H. 255
Twentieth Century Group *7*
Twentieth Century Society 178
Twickenham, Fieldend, Strawberry Hill *78, 79*
Tyne pedestrian and cycle tunnels *250*, 251

underground stations, Loughton Station, Essex 246, *247*
Uni-Seco Structures Ltd 102
United Shopfitters of Bristol 209
universities
Durham University *134*, 135
Free University, Berlin 19
Liverpool University 5, 242, *243*
Sheffield University 18
Southampton University 18, 144, *145*
St Catherine's College, University of Oxford 19, 152, *153*
Swansea University *146*, 147
University of Cambridge *150*, 151
University of Hertfordshire 128, *129*
University of York 17
Uren, Reginald 201

van Tijen, Willem *5*
Varin, René 265
Ventris, Michael 11
Vienna *5*
village signs *30*, 31
Vincent & Gorbing 128
Vincent, Leonard 197

Wachsmann, Konrad 10
Wagner, Otto *5*
Walker, Brenda 48
Walls, H.F. 206
Walsall, West Midlands, Memorial Gardens 156, *157*
war rationing 9–10
Ward, Basil 6
Ward, Edmund 148
Wates Estates 92
Watford, Hertfordshire, Odhams Press Hall *192*, 193
Watson, James Paton 202
Weedon, Harry 217
Weekend Review 91
Weeks, David 206
Weißenhofsiedlung, Stuttgart *6*
Welwyn Garden City, Hertfordshire, Templewood School *130*, 131
Whitfield, William 135
Whiting, Penelope 44
William Halcrow & Partners 222
Williams & Williams 18
Williams, Alfred 106
Wilson House, Lasswade, Lothian *66, 67*
'windowgrid' 18
windows 16
neoprene gaskets 18
Wisbech, Norfolk, Swedish prefabs, Marshland St James *104*, 105
Woman's Journal, House of the Year 17, *76*
Womersley, Peter 51, *59*
wood 9–10
Worcester, Odeon Cinema *216*, 217
Wright, Frank Lloyd 9, 52, 80, 96
Wyld, Ross 160
Wynne, David 164

Yates, Cook and Darbyshire 193
Yates, Peter 68, 117
YMCA Indian Student Hostel, London 136, *137*
York
Festival of Britain 13
University of York 17
Yorke, F.R.S. *7–8*, 13, 24, 44
Yorke, Rosenberg and Mardall 24, 44, 105
Yorke, Thelma 44
Youngman, Peter 278

Zeitgeist 6

PICTURE CREDITS

All photographs © Elain Harwood, except the following:
15, 50 Arcaid Images / Alamy Stock Photo
20 Chronicle / Alamy Stock Photo
23 akg-images / VIEW Pictures / Dennis Gilbert
25, 58, 81, 130, 158 © Historic England Archive
39 Morley von Sternberg / Riba Collections
77 © Philip Sayer
89 James Morris – VIEW / Alamy Stock Photo
116 © Howard Morris / GreyScape (www.greyscape.com)
223 Rosey / Alamy Stock Photo
232 Sam Mellish / Getty
250 Alan Dawson / Alamy Stock Photo